I0817513

VINTAGE COUNTRY

A COWBOY'S SWEET
by
PATSY MONTANA

★ TONY RUSSELL ★

4880 Lower Valley Road • Atglen, PA 19310

Elephant Book Company Limited
Purcell, St. Mary's Hall
Rawstorn Road
Colchester
Essex, CO3 3JH
United Kingdom
www.elephantbookcompany.com

Copyright © Elephant Book Company Limited 2025

All rights reserved. No part of this work may be reproduced or used in any form or by any means—graphic, electronic, or mechanical, including photocopying or information storage and retrieval systems—without written permission from the publisher.

The scanning, uploading, and distribution of this book or any part thereof via the Internet or any other means without the permission of the publisher is illegal and punishable by law. Please purchase only authorized editions and do not participate in or encourage the electronic piracy of copyrighted materials.

"Schiffer," "Schiffer Publishing, Ltd.," and the pen and inkwell logo are registered trademarks of Schiffer Publishing, Ltd.

Editorial director: Will Steeds
Project manager: Tom Seabrook
Executive editor: Laura Ward
Book & cover design: Paul Palmer-Edwards
Reproduction: Pixel Colour Imaging Ltd

ISBN: 978-0-7643-6968-1
Printed in China

Published by Schiffer Publishing, Ltd.
4880 Lower Valley Road
Atglen, PA 19310
Phone: (610) 593-1777; Fax: (610) 593-2002
Email: Info@schifferbooks.com
Web: www.schifferbooks.com

For our complete selection of fine books on this and related subjects, please visit our website at www.schifferbooks.com. You may also write for a free catalog.

Schiffer Publishing's titles are available at special discounts for bulk purchases for sales promotions or premiums. Special editions, including personalized covers, corporate imprints, and excerpts, can be created in large quantities for special needs. For more information, contact the publisher.

We are always looking for people to write books on new and related subjects. If you have an idea for a book, please contact us at proposals@schifferbooks.com

Every effort has been made to trace the copyright holders of the artworks in this book but one or two have proved unreachable. Elephant Book Company would be grateful if the artists concerned would contact them, in order for any errors or omissions to be corrected in future editions.

CONTENTS

FOREWORD

by Scott B. Bomar

Roni Stoneman, the youngest daughter of influential early recording pioneer Ernest V. "Pop" Stoneman, used to tell a funny story about her father. She would recount a conversation he had with a man who just discovered that Pop's wife, Hattie, had given birth to twenty-three children, including several sets of twins. The man asked, "Pop, did you get twins every time?" The elder Stoneman grinned and replied, "No, there were thousands of times we didn't get *anything*."

It's the kind of story that transforms Ernest Stoneman from a name on a dusty old 78 rpm record into a real man who had not only talent but a wicked sense of humor. In many ways, that quest for illumination—from mere historical figure to vibrant artist—has been Tony Russell's lifelong work as a music historian, scholar, author, discographer, and ardent champion of 78s. Though meticulous in his approach, Tony's quest for information about the artists who shaped early country music has never been an exercise in academic minutiae. Instead, he seeks to keep these artists alive by contributing to the preservation of their legacies for future generations. Even his *Country Music Records: A Discography, 1921–1942*, considered the definitive reference source for pre–World War II country recordings, is an engaging read. What should be a dry and straightforward compilation of data manages to crackle with life, thanks to the author's deep love for his subject. Tony Russell may appear to be a researcher, but he's actually a storyteller.

As a hopelessly irredeemable roots music nerd obsessed with such stories, I often find myself unable to resist the urge to purchase one of the always expensive but frequently revelatory CD box sets compiled by Bear Family Records in Germany. I am particularly drawn to the extensive in-depth album notes, and I first began to truly appreciate Tony Russell after reading his

Though the image is from the ’60s, this is how “Pop” Stoneman started out forty years earlier—as a one-man band playing autoharp and harmonica.

words in the books accompanying the sets compiling the historically important Bristol and Johnson City sessions. I've admired him from a distance ever since. Tony and coauthor Ted Olson detailed the lives of the performers in a way that made the music even more exciting to hear. And isn't that the point?

I'm laughing to myself as I'm reminded of a night when I was in bed reading a particularly oversized volume about music—perhaps it was the Beatles *Anthology* or some similarly gigantic music encyclopedia—when my wife walked in and joked, "You know, music is for listening to, not just reading about, right?" Touché. I still contend that the next best thing to listening to music is reading about it. And maybe the very best thing is reading something that makes me want to get up and hear that music right away.

That's what Tony Russell's *Vintage Country* does for me. While reading through this book, I kept getting sidetracked by the overwhelming desire to hear a recording he recommended. Since I don't happen to have a jaw-droppingly expensive collection of the rarest 78 records on the planet, I was pleased to find that many of these recordings are available on Spotify or YouTube. Tony has done an excellent job recommending recordings that reflect the wide variety of styles that "country" music encompassed in its early years. And I don't think he'd mind that I set his book down for frequent trips to the computer to experience the music about which he is so passionate, and to appreciate its diversity.

In my own work as a historian and author, I am most known for my focus on country and roots music, particularly the Bakersfield Sound and West Coast country of the 1950s and '60s. That music, of course, didn't evolve in a vacuum. For me to best understand its significance, I must grasp what came before. That's why I'm so grateful for Tony's important work across the decades in illuminating the building blocks of country music's origins as a commercial enterprise. But as that hopelessly irredeemable roots music nerd that I am, I also think Tony's writing is . . . fun! Whether you consider yourself a historian or a casual fan, Tony manages to beautifully bridge that gap. That's because, though he has my undying respect as a scholar, I recognize a fellow fan when I see one. Never academically condescending or pedantic, Tony is a genuinely humble and generous researcher who simply loves the music and wants to share that love with the rest of us.

Growing up as a music obsessive in the pre-internet era, I relied on books like this to learn more about artists I loved and to be introduced to artists I would grow to love. With the rise of the internet, such reference works fell out of favor among book publishers, and I was really sorry to see them go. Over time, my generation has become nostalgic for these kinds of books. At the same time, younger generations have found themselves drawn to Polaroid cameras, vinyl records, and, yes, even physical books as important reference sources. I believe this phenomenon reflects an innate desire to connect with and understand our collective cultural past, specifically through understanding tangible media. And what's more tangible than books and old records? I'm glad that both are back, and a huge smile is spreading across my face as I'm imagining a kid reading this book and then hearing a vintage Pops Stoneman recording for the first time.

In case you couldn't tell, I'm not only a music fan. I'm a big Tony Russell fan. I know you're going to enjoy *Vintage Country* as much as I did. You might read it cover to cover, or you might skip around to read up on some of your favorite artists—or to learn about some you haven't yet discovered. Either way, I promise this is a book you'll return to multiple times, and it's a book that, most importantly, will send you down some fun musical rabbit holes. Enjoy reading and enjoy listening. Because, again, that's the point!

Scott B. Bomar
Los Angeles
January 2025

INTRODUCTION

This book is about music largely made by and for working people, for recreation, remembrance, and release; to cope with the present, revisit the past, and face the future. Around a hundred years ago—in 1920, say—it was everywhere.

You could hear it in schoolhouses and town halls. At store openings, school breakings, and election rallies. At picnics and ice-cream suppers, parties and dances, fiddlers' conventions and all-day singings. You might catch it in the street or the courthouse square. It was played in people's houses, or on their porches, for the entertainment of family and friends. It had no name. It was just "music."

And it was everywhere geographically too. No one place owned it. Because of its subsequent history, you may think that this music is somehow intrinsically Southern, but you would be mistaken. It was part of everyday life in Southwestern cow towns, Midwestern farming communities, and every other region of the United States.

By present-day standards, the world of 1920 was starved of information and communication. No internet, no cell phones, no TV or radio. Local newspapers served only the literate. Even for automobile owners, transportation was problematic: Many rural communities could be reached only by dirt roads, if at all. If you wanted to hear music, you rode or walked into town, or you made it yourself.

But some twenty years earlier, around the turn of the nineteenth century into the twentieth, a new piece of technology had arrived to present a third way. The phonograph changed forever the experience of *listening*. Inscribed in the groove of a wax cylinder or shellac disc, music—or speech, or birdsong, or any sound whatsoever—could be freed from the inexorable grasp of time and *played back*. The recorded performance lived in a perpetual present, unalterable and (if looked after carefully) virtually indestructible.

This change did not come cheap. Disc records (which became the industry standard) cost seventy-five cents—possibly a day's wage for a farmhand or a

In the early twentieth century, there were thousands of musicians making what would one day be called country music. Many, like these, are unidentified figures in old photographs.

Okeh launched its "Old Time Tunes" catalog in 1925, following the example of its rival Columbia, which had initiated its "Old Familiar Tunes" list the year before.

millworker. The phonographs to play them on were expensive items of domestic furniture. Nevertheless, the opportunity to possess your own entertainment, rather than rely on others to provide it, proved irresistible. People in remote communities, making rare trips to town for seed, flour, sugar, coffee, and other staples to support them for a season, found time to visit a music store and acquire newly released records, which might be their only sources of musical diversion for months.

What records could they buy? (We are still in 1920.) Popular songs delivered by professional stage or studio vocalists. Popular dance tunes played by orchestras. Songs and comedy routines dating from the late-nineteenth-century minstrel stage. Hits from the New York theater. Songs from "the old country" in Italian, Greek, Norwegian, Yiddish—all the languages of immigrant America. Sermons and political speeches. Newer strains like Hawaiian guitar music and jazz. The first records of the blues.

Areas of musical interest and taste were already marked out. The army of talent scouts, producers, publicists, distributors, and retailers that constituted the record trade was confidently advancing on many fronts, offering different musics to different sections of their audience. Jigs and reels on fiddle or accordion for Irish Americans. The laments called *amanes* that engrossed Greek and Turkish Americans. Gospel quartets for the devout and saucy comic songs for the profane. African American blues for what the trade then called "the Race."

Faced with this variety, retailers needed a way of distinguishing between the records they could sell and those for which they had no customers. A music store owner in Boston's Irish section or New York's Little Italy obviously had a different clientele from one in St. Louis, Memphis, or Atlanta. So the record companies began to group their releases in genre-specific catalogs, each with its own numbering system: Popular and Dance records here, Syrian or Swedish records there. Sacred Selections. Race Records. And, from about 1925, Old Time Tunes.

To understand what this last term meant, and why it required a separate catalog, we must drop in on 1923, the year the record business began to pay serious attention to a phenomenon it hadn't been aware of: the existence of a market for ostensibly rural and small-town music. Old-time fiddling, Old World ballads, Victorian parlor songs, folk songs of the Southern mountains, narratives of Western cowboy life, harmonica novelties imitating trains or foxhunts, and, especially, the music of bands using fiddle, banjo, mandolin, guitar, and other stringed instruments.

The recording men's first tentative forays into this world surprised them. They discovered that customers across the nation would readily shell out for these early records of Fiddlin' John Carson, Henry Whitter, Ernest V. Stoneman, or Eck Robertson. But, at this point, the industry had very little notion of what it was dealing with. To most of the recording managers, these stories of train wrecks and kicking mules were almost as foreign as the stuff they were selling to their non-Anglophone customers in their own languages. For two or three years, they recorded this unfamiliar music haphazardly, sometimes inexpertly, giving it no special treatment. But the sales continued to be steady, and perceptive producers like Ralph S. Peer at Victor Records and Frank B. Walker at Columbia realized that this material was not just marketable but of extraordinary richness and variety—and so, potentially, even more marketable. They were the first to create discrete catalogs called "Old Time Tunes," or "Old Time Songs," "Old Familiar Tunes," "Native American Melodies," "Songs from Dixie" . . . each record label had its own descriptive term.

Now there's a point to this talk of catalogs and numerical series. It wasn't just the business of filing clerks. With their policies and activities now accurately directed toward defined markets, the recording men had clear to-do lists. Each season, they needed to restock their old-time catalog with records of fiddling, mountain ballads, tragedy songs, rustic comic sketches, and so on, and their "Race" list with blues, jazz, jug band tunes, and hokum novelties. They went about this task with energy, and in doing so they gave a voice to innumerable musicians whom we today cannot imagine being absent from our collective listening experience. But they also revised history. Some of the music that used to be sung and played was now judged to be unmarketable. You will look for a long time for records of the Appalachian dulcimer, or stringbands using a cello (as once many did), or any nonsacred unaccompanied singing. The business acquired a bias toward stringbands and singing guitarists, and, within a few years, that hardened into a definition.

But as well as editing history, the parallel catalogs created a new kind of segregation.

In 1930, Victor promoted its old-time records with images of barefoot mountaineers and moonshine jugs. By the mid-'30s, Decca Records had moved away from such stereotypes to depict instead some of the stars in its roster of "Hill Billy" artists.

THERE'S a lot of wonderful entertainment in the releases of Vocalion Old-Time Tunes for September. Happy Bud Harrison, Dixie's favorite entertainer, amazes you with his Levee Breaking Blues. Then Floyd Thompson and His Home Towners play an old one in a new way. Remember "Red Wing?" And there's a host of others. See the list of the latest issues on the next page.

Then go over the complete list of Vocalion Old-Time Tunes. You'll find just the kind of entertainment you've been looking for—all the old favorites that will never die—sacred numbers, barn dances, the soul-stirring melodies of Dixie, just the music you want to hear is included in the list of Vocalion Old-Time Tunes.

Come in and ask us to play them for you. You'll be as delighted to hear them as we are to play them for you.

Vocalion Records issued a monthly "Almanac" describing its new releases. Featured this month were a Mississippi blue yodeler who wasn't Jimmie Rodgers, and a stringband from Indianapolis.

It's a historical fact that Black and white musical forms had coexisted for a century or more before the phonograph, each expanding and enlivening the other. But this musical confederacy would not be represented in the twentieth century, on these records neatly arranged in their different catalogs. Because once you distinguish, you divide. Between old-time and "Race," there now ran a fence that became a cultural demarcation line. African American musicians who could play old-time music—and there were many—were diverted to the "Race" list, where to survive they might have to become guitar- or piano-playing blues singers. The complex, heterogeneous backstory of vernacular music was suppressed. It was all too diffuse, too racially ambiguous, too tricky to promote and sell.

Old-time music, a genre birthed and named by the industry, bore that title through the 1920s and into the Depression years, but gradually—and not without protest from some participants—it acquired a new name, "hillbilly." It wasn't until the '40s that the music business began to call it "country and western" or simply "country music." It was essentially the same product, modified and modernized yet still recognizable to performers who had been there since the start. It might have lost some of its regional characteristics and become Pan-American, but enough continuities remained to keep the music on track and its audience on board.

So this is the music that gives this book its title. *Country*—from its recorded beginnings as old-time music in the 1920s up to the '50s (and beyond). And *Vintage* because everyone in the book had at least their first record released in the then-standard format of the 10 inch 78 rpm disc. This isn't an antiquarian gesture on the author's part: the heyday of the 78 does actually correspond to, and define, a period when country music had a keen sense of itself in relation to its past—an awareness that unites Jimmie Rodgers and Hank Williams, Patsy Montana and Patsy Cline.

Country music didn't immediately change just because the record industry preferred vinyl to shellac, or 45 to 78, but other shifts—social, musical, and commercial—did begin about this time that somewhat altered the character of country music, distancing it a little from origins that were beginning to be regarded, by certain figures in the musical establishment, as antiquated, embarrassing—not Nashville but Poor-white-trashville.

But to return to *Vintage Country* and its contents: I said before that it went up to the '50s, but added "and beyond" because many artists prolonged their careers beyond 78s into the age of the 45 and the LP; some, like Ralph Stanley, went on working beyond even that, to the end of the twentieth century and into the next millennium.

Several of the artists included here are famous, like Jimmie Rodgers, the Carter Family, or Hank Williams; many are not, but that tells us less about the quality of their music than about the vagaries of history and the priorities of commerce. Part of this book's purpose is to restore these overlooked figures to the country music narrative, by telling their stories and highlighting songs and tunes that represent their talent, their inventiveness, and their often arresting individuality.

So the book is itself a kind of catalog—but not, of course, an exhaustive one. In the period we're concerned with, thousands of musicians were involved in old-time/hillbilly/country music, and their recordings must number many tens of thousands. No book could contain all that; no coffee table could sustain its weight.

Vintage Country identifies as "Key Recordings" over 550 songs and tunes by slightly more than a hundred artists. So this is a selection, and necessarily a personal one. Books aren't written by committees. (I grant you the King James Bible.) Some readers may feel that I've spurned the claims of *X* while elevating those of *Y*, or may challenge my choice of songs by *Z*. If so, I'm sorry, but not very, because differences of opinion provoke debate, and I hope this book encourages readers to listen to, and talk about—and disagree about—and investigate this fascinating and many-sided music.

But not because it's quaint, or because it gives off a pleasingly musty aroma of old times. The musicians who made it would not thank you for such condescension. They didn't sing and play as they did or spend their lives in rickety buses, crisscrossing the country to earn a living, so that they could become charming postcards in a scrapbook or have their records locked away in bank vaults as investment-quality rarities. Many of them could not foresee LPs or CDs, let alone the immense library of music provided by online platforms. But if they *had* known, they would have been happy that by these means their music would be heard as clearly in 2025 as when it

By 1940, the role of presenting country music to consumers had largely been transferred from records to radio. WLS in Chicago's annual souvenir album was full of news and pictures of the men and women heard on this powerful station.

was made in 1925—and far more widely. They would have been pleased that they still mattered, that the world still cared.

Of course, there was more music being made than what got onto records, but it has all faded into the ether, gone with the wind. All we can ever know is the music that records preserved, the music that survives. Thankfully, there is a great deal of it, and you can spend a long, pleasurable, and immensely rewarding time discovering it, perhaps learning to play it, always enjoying it. I hope *Vintage Country* inspires you to do all of that.

Jimmie Rodgers

OLD-TIME MUSIC
1923 TO THE DEPRESSION

"The fiddle and guitar craze is sweeping northwards!" bawled a 1924 ad for records by **Gid Tanner** and **Riley Puckett**. Soon, these newly uncovered sounds had their own niche in record stores and catalogs, and, throughout the decade, recording crews chased each other around the South and Southwest, setting up location sessions in Atlanta or Charlotte, Memphis or Dallas, to capture regional music. The pursuit slackened in the early '30s, but by then the leading labels—Victor, Columbia, Okeh, and Brunswick—had gathered thousands of recordings of fiddling, singing, stringbands, gospel quartets, banjo pickers, Hawaiian-style guitarists, and the other riches of old-time music.

FIDDLIN' JOHN CARSON

Dates: John William Carson, b. March 23, 1874, Blue Ridge, GA; d. December 11, 1949, Decatur, GA
Instruments: fiddle, vocals
Recording Debut: June 1923

KEY RECORDINGS

The Little Old Log Cabin in the Lane, **1923**
The Old Hen Cackled and the Rooster's Going to Crow, **1923**
You Will Never Miss Your Mother Until She Is Gone, **1923, 1929, 1934**
The Farmer Is the Man That Feeds Them All, **1923, 1934**
Gonna Swing on the Golden Gate, **1927**

On or about June 14, 1923, John Carson, a forty-nine-year-old cotton mill worker, house painter, and popular entertainer, stood in an improvised studio in downtown Atlanta and fiddled and sang a couple of antique pieces into a microphone. The studio is gone (demolished in 2019 to make room for a Margaritaville) but the performances survive, since Carson was not broadcasting but recording: creating, on Okeh Record 4890, "The Little Old Log Cabin in the Lane" and "The Old Hen Cackled and the Rooster's Going to Crow," what historians generally recognize as the first disc of songs in the idiom then called "old-time," now "country music."

It's fitting that this honor is his, because he had been a significant figure in the musical history of the South for over a decade, and he remained so for years afterward. His ebullient personality as much as his skill ensured frequent victories at fiddlers' contests, and he was a favorite on the Atlanta radio station WSB. On records, he provided Okeh with more than a hundred songs—ballads, fiddle tunes, and comic novelties, a catalog ranging from "The Honest Farmer" and "I'm Glad My Wife's in Europe" to "Papa's Billy Goat" and "Casey Jones." At first, he recorded on his own, then with his guitar-playing daughter, Rosa Lee (1911–92), who, in the guise of "Moonshine Kate," engaged him in pert repartee. Further musicians were added to constitute the Virginia Reelers, including the tearaway fiddler Earl Johnson (1886–1965), who steers "Hell Bound for Alabama" as if taking the title literally. (Johnson's own records are full of incandescent fiddling.)

Like many first-wave recording artists, Carson was judged old-fashioned by the time of the Depression, but in 1934 Bluebird Records brought him and "Kate" back for a farewell session, bantering as vivaciously as ever.

Polk C. Brockman, who published Carson's songbook in the '30s, was the Atlanta entrepreneur who had the idea of getting him onto Okeh Records in 1923—a key event in the creation of the country music business.

"ECK" ROBERTSON

Dates: Alexander Campbell Robertson, b. November 20, 1887, Madison County, AR; d. February 15, 1975, Borger, TX
Instrument: fiddle
Recording Debut: June 30, 1922

KEY RECORDINGS

Arkansaw Traveler [with Henry C. Gilliland], **1922**
Sallie Gooden [solo], **1922**
Ragtime Annie [solo], **1922**
There's a Brown Skin Girl Down the Road Somewhere, **1929**
Brilliancy Medley, **1929**

You could argue that this entry should have come first. "Eck" Robertson and his partner Henry C. Gilliland made records almost a year before **Fiddlin' John Carson**. Their release was delayed, but when "Arkansaw Traveler" and "Sallie Gooden" arrived in record stores in April 1923, Carson was still two months away from entering a studio. But Robertson and Gilliland were fiddlers, playing tunes for dances and at fiddlers' contests, and this, though it may have seemed otherwise at the time, was not the road that old-time music would take. It would primarily be an idiom not of tunes but of songs.

So it's Carson, the first musician to record a song, whom we should credit (as I have) with opening the century-long festival we now call country music. But historians differ on the matter, and lovers of old-time music are free to make a comparable case for Robertson and Gilliland, perhaps submitting as evidence the former's unaccompanied solo recording of "Sallie Gooden," a display of technique, variation, and vivacity way beyond the powers of the Georgia fiddler.

Gilliland, who had been the older partner by forty-two years, died in 1924, but Robertson lived on, at the heart of Texan old-time music, for another half century, working as a piano tuner and repairman, playing at fiddlers' contests, and leading a family band with his wife, Nettie, and some of their children. He often sported a goatee that made him look like the popular representation of "Uncle Sam." Fifteen years after his original "Sallie Gooden," he was reported to be still "scorching the air" with it. But he was discontented about his legacy, feeling he hadn't received enough credit either for his being there at the start of it all or for the fertile invention he had brought to the art of old-time fiddling.

INSTRUMENTAL RECORDS

18956 { **Sallie Gooden** — A. C. (Eck) Robertson
10-in. list price 75c. { **Arkansaw Traveler** — Henry C. Gilliland-A. C. (Eck) Robertson

One day, not so many months ago, two Southwesterners blew into our laboratory and told us they could play the fiddle. Now we know an awful lot of people who can play the fiddle, so we weren't impressed. Here is their first record. Eck made "Sallie Gooden" alone—a medley of jigs and reels, in the very best style of the travelling cowboy fiddler, with almost continuous double-stopping, one string being used for a kind of bag-pipe drone-bass, and the other to carry the melody. In both numbers there is no accompaniment, none being needed. In the Arkansaw Traveler, you will realize there are two of a kind, for Gilliland gets to it in as business-like a style as his partner.

19014 { **Liebesfreud** — George Hamilton Green
10-in. list price 75c. { **Fair Rosmarin** — George Hamilton Green

Simply to slambang a xylophone for dancers, half-lost among the hootings of a jazz orchestra, is no test for any master of this difficult instrument. So George Hamilton Green, therefore, the famous xylophonist of the All Star Trio and other organizations, is making two records for us, as soloist with an orchestral accompaniment. Furthermore, he is not interpreting low-grade music, but two compositions of Fritz Kreisler's own, based on old Viennese airs. Both numbers are old Vienna waltzes, and although primarily concert numbers, skilful dancers, or "old fashioned" ones, which amounts to the same thing, will be interested to try them out. The long shivery tremolo of the instrument adapts itself very well to sustained passages, and its icy tinkle, its trills and scales, give the compositions brilliancy.

8

Always use the Tungs-tone Stylus in playing Victor Records.

A Victor copywriter tells the story behind the first record of Southwestern fidding. At the time, Robertson was working as a piano tuner and salesman in Vernon, Texas, and Gilliland as a justice officer for the nearby city of Altus, Oklahoma.

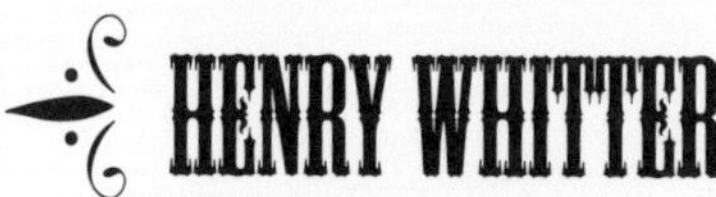

HENRY WHITTER

Dates: William Henry Whitter, b. April 6, 1892, Carroll County, VA; d. November 17, 1941, Morganton, NC
Instruments: harmonica, guitar, vocals
Recording Debut: December 1923

KEY RECORDINGS

Wreck on the Southern Old 97, **1923**
Lost Train Blues, **1923**
The Old Time Fox Chase, **1923**
Lonesome Road Blues, **1923**
A Pretty Gal's Love [with Fisher Hendley and Marshall Small], **1930**

In his youth, Henry Whitter worked in a cotton mill in Fries, Virginia, and his first music making was probably for fellow operatives, playing as a one-man band with guitar and rack harmonica and delivering old-time numbers like "Little Brown Jug" or "The New River Train." By 1923, when executives in the Northern phonograph industry began looking South for talent, he was judged worthy of recording.

According to Whitter himself, he first took the train to New York and Okeh's studio in March 1923—three and a half months before **Fiddlin' John Carson** made *his* first record. It's possible that he made undocumented tests, but it wasn't until December that he produced issuable recordings, among them the railroad ditty "Wreck on the Southern Old 97" and a couple of harmonica solos imitating trains and foxhunting hounds. With so little Southern vernacular music available on record, these discs sold in tens—maybe hundreds—of thousands. They also prompted other Southern musicians to aspire to a recording career. **Ernest V. Stoneman**, unimpressed, offered himself to Okeh as a superior performer. "Henry was just merely a very amateurish musician," he opined, "and he sung through his nose something terrible." One wonders if he had ever heard Whitter's recording of "Wild Bill Jones" with **Kelly Harrell**, on which Harrell sings in one key and Whitter accompanies him in another—throughout. (Stoneman did commend Whitter for his fair treatment of fellow musicians.)

Apart from a few tunes with a trio, such as "'Round-Town Girl," which are among the earliest old-time stringband recordings, Whitter mainly worked solo until 1927, when he teamed with the singing fiddler **G. B. Grayson** to make music of another order altogether. At personal appearances he was billed as a "famous music writer and radio entertainer," and he maintained this professional status into the 1930s, now based in North Carolina.

Henry Whitter unashamedly promoted himself as "the outstanding harmonica and guitar artist of the present age." It's not a verdict anyone now would echo, but it was, after all, early days.

GID TANNER

Dates: James Gideon Tanner, b. June 6, 1885, Walton County, GA; d. May 13, 1960, Barrow County, GA
Instruments: fiddle, banjo, vocals
Recording Debut: March 17, 1924

KEY RECORDINGS

I'm Satisfied, **1924, 1934**
Just Gimme the Leavings, **1925**
You've Got to Stop Drinking Shine, **1930**
Down Yonder, **1934**
Back Up and Push, **1934**

It was part of the theatricality of the old-time fiddlers' contest that there should be fierce rivalries, even if they were fictitious ones. In 1913, questioned by a reporter about **Fiddlin' John Carson**, Gid Tanner allowed, "He's fancy on singing and dancing and cutting up jack generally, but I can beat him a mile on straight fiddling. All my folks was fiddlers, and good fiddlers too." The two men were still at genial loggerheads more than a decade later, but by then they were recording stars with their own bands (on rival labels, of course).

Tanner's nominal leadership of **the Skillet-Lickers** made him one of the best-known figures in 1920s old-time music, but the group setting generally confined him to background singing and playing and noises-off. Yet, this was the man whom newspapers had once dubbed "Laughin' Gid Tanner," "the big, red-faced chap who sings bass and falsetto and fiddles," "a show by himself." An Alabama paper in 1924 reported on "his fiddling and singing of 'I'm Satisfied' and 'Boll Weevil' bringing down the house." Three months before, he had put those two songs on his debut record.

Over the next few years, Tanner would occasionally step out from the shadow of the Skillet-Lickers and present the record buyer with undiluted Gid, as on the minstrel number "Just Gimme the Leavings" or the banjo-accompanied "You Got to Stop Drinking Shine." His last recordings, made in 1934 with a lineup of the Skillet-Lickers undominated by **Clayton McMichen**, gave him unaccustomed room to maneuver, and it's a delight to hear him joyfully chanting old comic songs like "Keep Your Gal at Home" and "I Ain't No Better Now." The earlier Skillet-Licker years had obscured the fact that Gid Tanner was one of the great vaudeville comedians of old-time country music.

Columbia initiated its "Old Familiar Tunes" catalog in late 1924. The "new process" of electrical recording began to be used the following year.

RILEY PUCKETT

Dates: George Riley Puckett,
b. May 7, 1894, Alpharetta, GA;
d. July 13, 1946, Fulton County, GA
Instruments: guitar, vocals
Recording Debut: March 7, 1924

KEY RECORDINGS

My Carolina Home [with Clayton McMichen], **1926**
Red River Valley [with Hugh Cross], **1927**
Waitin' for the Evenin' Mail, **1934**
Ragged but Right, **1934**
'Way Out There, **1939**

With his first recordings, in 1924–25, Riley Puckett gave Columbia Records a rich selection of old-time Southern songs like "Old Black Joe" and "O! Susanna," delivered in a strong yet sensitive voice that recorded well. You wouldn't guess, hearing them, that he was also the first great guitarist in country music, but with the formation of **the Skillet-Lickers** as a recording band in 1926, Puckett was revealed as a picking phenomenon. Contemporaries who played guitar, such as **Henry Whitter** or **Ernest V. Stoneman**, were rhythm keepers, no more; Puckett, with his jaw-dropping, time-shifting runs, was in a different league. In 1927, he recorded a guitar solo, "Fuzzy Rag," introducing it, "Well, hello, folks, here we are once again! I've got several letters and requests wishing to hear me pick the guitar alone. . . . Now pay close attention to these runs!" On the other side, "The Darkey's Wail," he gave an impression of African American slide guitar playing. In the dawn of recorded country music, it was a striking testament to that music's mixed heritage.

But it was his golden voice that sold records—with the Skillet-Lickers, **Clayton McMichen**'s Melody Men, and other pickup groups, as well as on solo numbers and vocal duets with McMichen or Hugh Cross. "My Carolina Home" shifted more than 260,000 copies, the third-best seller in Columbia's "Old Familiar Tunes" list. When his Columbia contract ended in 1931, he left Georgia, worked in radio in half a dozen cities, and recorded busily for Bluebird and Decca, applying his gorgeous, infinitely flexible voice to all kinds of songs, but especially pop numbers of the day like "Red Sails in the Sunset" or "When I Grow Too Old to Dream." If "crossover" had been a concept back then, Riley Puckett would have embodied it.

Riley Puckett with his art deco steel-bodied guitar in the studio of WNOX in Knoxville, Tennessee. Launched in 1921, WNOX was one of the oldest stations in the USA and for decades a vigorous promoter of country music.

UNCLE DAVE MACON

Dates: David Harrison Macon,
b. October 7, 1870, near McMinnville, TN;
d. March 22, 1952, Murfreesboro, TN
Instruments: banjo, vocals
Recording Debut: July 8, 1924

KEY RECORDINGS

(I'll) Keep My Skillet Good and Greasy, **1924**, **1935**
Chewing Gum, **1924**
Way Down the Old Plank Road, **1926**
Rock About My Sara Jane, **1927**
Buddy Won't You Roll Down the Line, **1928**

Uncle Dave Macon is one of country music's protean figures. At first glance, his jollity and jaunty banjo playing, his straw hats and bib-and-brace overalls, his cackling tales of country courtship and country ham seem to epitomize what the *Grand Ole Opry*, his radio home for years, purveyed as Southern rusticity—old-time music in its default mode. But his legacy of almost two hundred recordings offers us a more complex figure. He made one of the first hillbilly blues records—titled, indeed, "Hill Billie Blues"—and his advertisements declared, "He Moans a Wicked Instrument and Sings Some Mean Blues!" He led one of the most vivacious stringbands of his era, billed as his Fruit Jar Drinkers. And he preserved a rich portfolio of songs from the long-gone minstrel stage—songs that the original minstrel performers never had the opportunity to etch into 78 rpm discs. (In Macon's youth, his father ran a hotel in Nashville where vaudeville and circus acts stayed, and the boy had free passes to their shows.) Above all, he seems to have grasped, in his fifties, what many artists half his age did not: the inherent dramatic possibilities of the phonograph, and its capacity not merely to duplicate the performance of a song or tune but to create, in pieces like the four-part sequence "Uncle Dave's Travels," three-minute playlets of songs, tunes, jokes, and commentary—musical comedy in miniature.

But this is only part of the picture. Macon lived to be eighty-one, yet all the time he spent in recording studios amounted to barely a month. What established "the Dixie Dewdrop" as the grand old man of country music was his convivial radio presence and decades of personal appearances, equipped with his trademark "twin banjos, plug hat, gold teeth . . . the struttin'est strutter that ever strutted a strut."

Uncle Dave Macon and guitarist "Smoky Mountain Glenn" Stagner on the stage of the *Grand Ole Opry* in the late '30s.

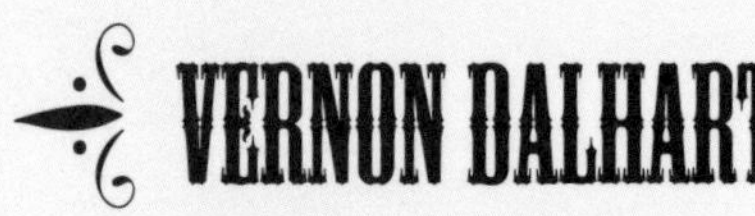

VERNON DALHART

Dates: Marion Try Slaughter,
b. April 6, 1883, Jefferson, TX;
d. September 15, 1948, Bridgeport, CT
Instruments: harmonica, vocals
Recording Debut: 1916

KEY RECORDINGS

Wreck of the Old 97, **1924**
The Prisoner's Song, **1924**
The Runaway Train, **1925, 1931**
The Letter Edged in Black, **1925**
The Death of Floyd Collins, **1925**
The John T. Scopes Trial, **1925**

Vernon Dalhart was one of a group of versatile men who worked in the recording studios of New York in the 1910s and early 1920s, turning out light classical melodies, operatic arias, and novelty songs for the young phonograph industry. His career took a swerve when, in 1924, he was commissioned by Victor to deliver a tale (recently premiered on Okeh by **Henry Whitter**) of a train disaster in Virginia, "Wreck of the Old 97." Coupling it with the lugubrious "Prisoner's Song," Victor advertised the record as "genuine songs of the Southern mountaineers, given with all their original lyric vigor and their quaint melody." The record sold a million for Victor alone and incalculably more on four dozen other labels, placing old-fashioned Southern music—of a kind—within reach of any American with a phonograph.

It's that "of a kind" that bothers some lovers of old-time music. Dalhart's accompaniments, invariably by studio musicians, were generally sedate, and much of his material was supplied by professional songwriters. A cultural comrade of **Fiddlin' John Carson** he assuredly wasn't. But the people who bought hillbilly records then—as distinct from those who collect them today—didn't care. His tales of death and disaster consistently outsold those delivered in more regionally characteristic voices, especially when the record labels masked him with rube pseudonyms like "Al Craver" or "Mack Allen." These were necessary disguises because, once Dalhart acquired a song, he would record it for anybody. In 1925–26, when a trapped Kentucky potholer was America's leading news story, Dalhart sang "The Death of Floyd Collins" on twenty-six labels.

When the hillbilly business revived in the mid-'30s, Dalhart's moralizing stories had lost their appeal. Perhaps, having seen the Depression wreck lives, people cared less about wrecked trains. He died forgotten by the industry he helped build.

Singing "hillbilly" songs was his most profitable recording work, but, unlike contemporaries such as Carson Robison, Vernon Dalhart never dressed the part, seeing himself instead as an all-round professional recordist.

FIDDLIN' POWERS

Dates: James Cowan Powers,
b. October 7, 1877, Castlewood, VA;
d. August 22, 1953, Abingdon, VA
Instrument: fiddle
Recording Debut: August 18, 1924

KEY RECORDINGS

Old Joe Clark, **1924**
Cripple Creek, **1924**
Ida Red, **1924**
Patty on the Turnpike, **1924**
Did You Ever See the Devil, Uncle Joe?, **1927**

In 1924, Cowan Powers placed first in a fiddlers' contest in Johnson City, Tennessee. Impressed, a local businessman arranged for the fiddler to be a phonograph star too. That August, at Victor's studios in Camden, New Jersey, "Fiddlin' Powers and Family"—son Charlie on banjo and daughters Carrie, Orpha, and Ada on guitar, mandolin, and ukulele, respectively—made records that Victor called "absolutely American music, sprung up in the hollows of the Southern Appalachian ranges." They conjured "memories of many a happy gathering in some little out-of-the-way place where the lights of the city never penetrate."

This is a milestone in the history of country music: the first discs by a working Appalachian stringband. Even in the thin atmosphere of acoustic recording, they have tremendous vigor. They sold so well that, two years later, Victor commissioned **Ernest Stoneman** to rerecord the same tunes by the new electrical process.

Cowan Powers was a farmer, carpenter, and leatherworker. "At that time," Ada remembered, "every young man in the county had to have an underarm holster. Now that tells you something about the times back then." Though locally renowned as a fiddler, he made music his trade only after his wife, Tilda, died; rather than leave his children while working elsewhere, he taught them to play music. Ada remembered them taking over $200 a night in the mining towns of Kentucky and West Virginia. They made more records, for Edison and Okeh, including "Old Virginia Reel," a charming two-part showcase of the children's talents and of the full band playing as if for a dance. "We retired in 1928," Ada said, "due to the matrimony bug," but Cowan Powers played on into the '50s—dying, according to legend, while playing one of his old numbers, "Cluck Old Hen," onstage with **the Stanley Brothers**.

Charlie, Ada, Orpha, and paterfamilias Cowan Powers present themselves to Victor Records' audience, 1924. The "vocal refrain" on "Old Joe Clark" was by studio pro Carson Robison.

ERNEST V. STONEMAN

Dates: Ernest Van Stoneman,
b. May 25, 1893, Monarat, VA;
d. June 14, 1968, Hermitage, TN
Instruments: harmonica, guitar, autoharp, vocals
Recording Debut: ca. September 4, 1924

KEY RECORDINGS

The Titanic, **1925**
All Go Hungry Hash House, **1926–28**
Kenny Wagner's Surrender, **1927**
The Story of the Mighty Mississippi, **1927**
The Mountaineer's Courtship, **1927**

Ernest Stoneman was an astute salesman, especially of himself. In 1924, perceiving a gap in the hardly formed old-time music business, he offered Okeh Records sturdy versions of topical songs and humorous ditties, accompanied on guitar or autoharp. Producer Ralph Peer was impressed by his savvy and, when he transferred to Victor Records in 1926, took Stoneman with him. By now, Stoneman had enlisted family—his wife, Hattie, on fiddle; brother George and brother-in-law Bolen Frost on banjos—and friends from Grayson and Carroll Counties, Virginia, like "Uncle" Eck Dunford and fiddler Kahle Brewer. They efficiently supplied Victor with sacred songs, rustic sketches like "Old Time Corn Shuckin'," Dunford's comic monologues, and stringband dance tunes. When Peer held his momentous recording session in Bristol, Tennessee, in 1927, where he would discover **Jimmie Rodgers** and **the Carter Family**, Stoneman's group was the first to be booked, and Stoneman himself was the focus of PR stories that Peer issued to the press, notably for his considerable earnings from record making ($3,600 in the previous year).

For a decade, Stoneman was one of old-time music's most reliable content providers, recording not only for Victor and Okeh but for Thomas Edison's label, and producing multiple versions of favorites like "Hand Me Down My Walking Cane," "Pass Around the Bottle," and "May I Sleep in Your Barn Tonight Mister." Altogether, he was responsible for over two hundred sides. In 1932, he moved his large family (thirteen children) to Washington, DC. His son Scotty later became known as a quick-fingered bluegrass fiddler, followed in that direction by his mandolin-playing sister, Donna. "Pop," as Ernest was now known, maintained the family group through many stylistic shifts in country music. He was the only artist to record in every technological form from wax cylinder to 78 rpm disc to long-playing album.

The Blue Ridge Corn Shuckers, Galax, Virginia, 1928. *Left to right*: Iver Edwards, George Stoneman, Eck Dunford, Ernest V. Stoneman, Hattie Stoneman, Bolen Frost. Most of these musicians were featured in both speaking and playing roles in the "rural dramas" "Old Time Corn Shuckin'," "Possum Trot School Exhibition," and "A Serenade in the Mountains."

THE HILL BILLIES

Instruments: fiddle, piano, guitar, ukulele, vocals
Recording Debut: January 15, 1925

KEY RECORDINGS
Old Joe Clark, **1925**
Cripple Creek, **1925–26**
Sally Ann, **1925–26**
(Old Time) Cinda, **1925–26**
Black Eyed Susie, **1927**
The Nine Pound Hammer, **1927**

Fiddlin' John Carson, Gid Tanner, Fiddlin' Powers—there's no mistaking what kind of men they were: deep-dyed, old-school Southerners, none too curious about other places and other ways. The Hill Billies, despite their name, were not like that. Though the Hopkins family had impeccable old-time-musical ancestry in Ashe County, North Carolina, the three brothers who created the band—Albert (1889–1932), piano; Joseph (1891–1939), guitar; John (1899–1974), ukulele—grew up in Washington, DC, where the family moved in the 1900s, their father employed in the US Census Bureau. The boys' youth would have been spent less in rustic pursuits than in absorbing and learning from the musical and theatrical culture of the nation's capital. When they secured a recording date in 1925, producer Ralph Peer asked, "What do you call yourselves?" They're supposed to have replied with a disarming "We're just a bunch of hillbillies." Some irony there.

Once the Hopkinses, with fiddler Elvis Alderman, had given their sponsors (first Okeh, then Brunswick) twenty-some spirited old-time dance tunes like "Cripple Creek" and "Sally Ann," they began to diversify. Waltzes, yodel songs, the vocal quartet "Hear Dem Bells," the special-effects number "The Nine Pound Hammer"; with a repertoire like this, the group expanded the already baggy definition of "old-time music," displaying it over the airwaves and in personal appearances through the Southeast. The shifting personnel included first-rate old-time musicians such as fiddler Charlie Bowman, banjoist Jack Reedy, and steel guitarist Frank Wilson, but the band did not survive the death of its leader, Al Hopkins, in 1932. The idea behind the group, however—versatile musicians playing a vaudevillian variety of old-time music—inspired similar organizations, such as the Blue Ridge Ramblers and the Blue Ridge Mountaineers, and created a template for the multitalented hillbilly radio bands of the '30s.

Al Hopkins's troupe created "hillbilly" stage sets for their vaudeville work. The steel guitarist featured here, Frank Wilson, was a pioneer of the instrument in country music. For their Brunswick records, the Hill Billies took on a new name, the Buckle Busters.

KELLY HARRELL

Dates: Crockett Kell(e)y Harrell,
b. September 13, 1889, Wythe County, VA;
d. July 9, 1942, Martinsville, VA
Instrument: vocals
Recording Debut: January 7, 1925

KEY RECORDINGS

Rovin' Gambler, **1925, 1926**
Butcher's Boy, **1925, 1926**
My Name Is John Johanna, **1927**
In the Shadow of the Pine, **1927**
Charles Giteau, **1927**
I'm Nobody's Darling on Earth, **1927**

Kelly Harrell spent his working life in the cotton-mill-strewn counties along the border of southwestern Virginia, first as a weaver, later as a loom fixer. From the 1910s, he worked at a mill in Fries, Virginia, where fellow mill hand **Henry Whitter** probably encouraged him to make contact with the Northern record companies that were seeking Southern talent. The two men cut some sides together for Okeh in 1925, but by then Harrell had introduced himself to Victor, who embarked on a two-year program of recording him singing well-loved folk songs of the region. Harrell proved to be an ideal teller of these old tales, his voice strong and clear, and the somewhat staid accompaniments by guitarist **Carson Robison** and a studio violinist did not prevent the records from selling well.

At this point, either Harrell himself or producer Ralph Peer made a case for having the singer backed by men from his own community: fiddler Posey Rorer, banjoist Raymond Hundley, and guitarist Alfred Steagall. The fruits of their collaboration, such as the hard-times narrative of "My Name Is John Johanna" and the gallows confession of "Charles Giteau" (actually Guiteau, who assassinated President James A. Garfield in 1881), were masterpieces of Southern storytelling and soberly beautiful stringband music. So too was an old song of lovers meeting and parting, "In the Shadow of the Pine," with its graceful segue from 4/4 into waltz time for the chorus, whose last line is accompanied only by a lonesome fiddle.

Harrell made a few more discs, demonstrating his versatility with sacred songs and a comic ditty about marital discord, "The Henpecked Man." By the standards of his time and place, he had been a successful recording artist, but he could not afford to quit millwork, and he died in harness, from a heart attack.

"Kelly Harrell has made two of the best records yet recorded of their kind . . . old time, backwoods songs, and splendidly sung and played."
Danville Bee, March 30, 1925

CHARLIE POOLE

Dates: Charles Cleveland Poole,
b. March 22, 1892, Randolph County, NC;
d. May 21, 1931, Rockingham, NC
Instruments: banjo, vocals
Recording Debut: July 27, 1925

KEY RECORDINGS

There'll Come a Time, **1926**
White House Blues, **1926**
Take a Drink on Me, **1927**
He Rambled, **1929**
Sweet Sunny South, **1929**
If the River Was Whisky, **1930**
Milwaukee Blues, **1930**

Charlie Poole burst on the world of recorded sound in 1925, singing and picking his banjo with demonic energy in the nonsensical bragging of "I'm the Man That Rode the Mule 'Round the World," then miraculously molding his voice, rough-edged as a corncob, around the sob story "Can I Sleep in Your Barn Tonight Mister." In his youth, he had listened to the minstrel songs and banjo tunes that filled the early disc catalogs, and in his own output, seventy-some recordings in five years, he gave them new and riotous life: comic capers like "Monkey on a String" and "Hungry Hash House"; homilies about the impermanence of life and love such as "There'll Come a Time," "Budded Rose," and "Old and Only in the Way." No old-time singer, not even **Uncle Dave Macon** or **Riley Puckett**, could match him in his command of different registers as he juggled jokes, tearjerkers, event ballads, and buoyant blues. He was fortunate in having excellent help: the superb fiddlers Posey Rorer, Lonnie Austin, and Odell Smith, and the impeccable guitarist Roy Harvey.

Poole's world was around present-day Eden, North Carolina, once a complex of small towns (Draper, Spray, Leaksville) near the Virginia line, a landscape littered with cotton mills. In the close quarters of the mill villages, musicians found each other and formed bands. Poole and his North Carolina Ramblers were merely the most celebrated in a community that embraced singer Walter Smith, banjoist Buster Carter, and guitarists Lewis McDaniel, Norman Woodlieff, and Preston Young, men for whom Poole lit the way to the recording studios.

Dead now for almost a century, and inexplicably overlooked by the Country Music Hall of Fame, Charlie Poole is still remembered with extraordinary fervor in Appalachia, and many of his songs have become staples of old-time country music and bluegrass.

Poole spent his youth working in cotton mills before finding more congenial employment as a musician.

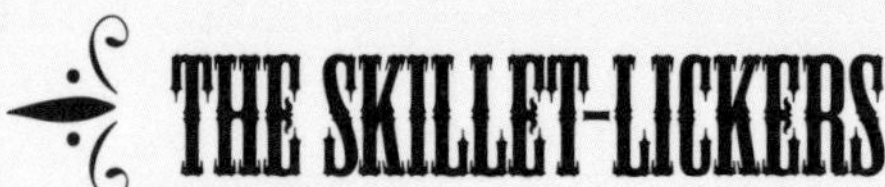

THE SKILLET-LICKERS

Instruments: fiddles, banjo, guitar, vocals
Recording Debut: April 17, 1926

KEY RECORDINGS

Bully of the Town, **1926**
Pass Around the Bottle and We'll All Take a Drink, **1926**
Watermelon on the Vine, **1926**
Liberty, **1928**
Sugar in the Gourd, **1930**
Molly Put the Kettle On, **1930**

"Skillet-Lickers" first appeared on a record label when Columbia started using it in 1926, but a circle of musicians around fiddler **Clayton McMichen** had been calling themselves the Lick Skillet Orchestra on WSB Atlanta for four years. ("Lickskillet" is a derisive expression for uncouth eating habits.) The term was co-opted for a band that Columbia's A&R man Frank Walker assembled from the Atlanta talent pool, with **Gid Tanner** as its nominal leader, plus McMichen, fiddlers Bert Layne (1889–1982) and later **Lowe Stokes**, banjoist Fate Norris (1878–1944), and guitarist/singer **Riley Puckett**. They were phenomenally successful. The four releases from their 1926 debut session sold, in total, more than half a million copies, and over the next five years a further fifty-some issues added another million.

These records were often of material that posterity tends to disregard: not the traditional hoedown tunes repossessed by stringband revivalists half a century later, but published "Southern" songs of the late nineteenth and early twentieth centuries such as "Alabama Jubilee" or "You Gotta Quit Kickin' My Dog Aroun'." The group also specialized in "rural dramas" like "A Corn Licker Still in Georgia," a multipart lye-soap opera of moonshine, music, and mayhem. The Skillet-Lickers' appeal lay in novel orchestration—twin- and triple-fiddle passages, prominent guitar, falsetto vocal harmony—and in Puckett's beguiling singing.

The Skillet-Lickers were a studio creation, and in public they often engaged other players. Despite its success, the group had internal stresses. McMichen, the youngest, had ambitions beyond old-time music, and the original lineup quit recording in 1931—to be succeeded in 1934 by a different configuration, with Tanner and his teenaged son Gordon on fiddles, Puckett, and mandolinist Ted Hawkins, defiantly old-timey but still exhilarating.

Columbia *"New Process"* Records
REG. U. S. PAT. OFF.

GID TANNER AND HIS SKILLET-LICKERS WITH RILEY PUCKETT AND CLAYTON McMICHEN

HERE'S a team indeed! It's a dance combination, and no high-stepping affair down their way draws the crowd like Gid and these pals of his, an all-star group.

It's not often you can have on one record three stars like Gid, Riley and Clayton, but Columbia offers them here.

GID TANNER AND HIS SKILLET-LICKERS WITH RILEY PUCKETT AND CLAYTON McMICHEN

Titles	Record No.
IT AIN'T GONNA' RAIN NO MO' THE ROVIN' GAMBLER—Vocals and Instrumentals	15447-D
MISSISSIPPI SAWYER GOING ON DOWN TOWN—Vocals and Instrumentals	15420-D
SHOW ME THE WAY TO GO HOME COTTON BAGGIN'—Vocals and Instrumentals	15404-D
NANCY ROLLIN OLD DAN TUCKER—Vocals and Instrumentals	15382-D
PRETTY LITTLE WIDOW LIBERTY—Vocals and Instrumentals	15334-D

VIVA-TONAL RECORDING. THE RECORDS WITHOUT SCRATCH

[13]

The group picture above shows Tanner, McMichen, Puckett, and banjoist Fate Norris, though by the time this catalog appeared, in 1929, further musicians had been added to the Skillet-Lickers.

UNCLE JIMMY THOMPSON

Dates: James Davis Thompson,
b. November 19, 1854, Putnam County, TN;
d. February 16, 1931, Laguardo, TN
Instrument: fiddle
Recording Debut: November 1, 1926

KEY RECORDINGS

Billy Wilson, **1926**
Karo, **1926**
Lynchburg, **1930**
Uncle Jimmy's Favorite Fiddling Pieces, **1930**

On a November evening in 1925, an elderly man sat at a microphone in Nashville radio station WSM. For two hours, he played tunes on his fiddle and reminisced to an announcer. The fiddler was Uncle Jimmy Thompson, the announcer George D. Hay, and between them they were laying the foundation stone of the nation's most famous country music show. Hay had come from Chicago, where he had created the WLS *National Barn Dance*, and the popularity of Thompson's broadcast encouraged him to give WSM a similar program. Within weeks, it had a name: the *Grand Ole Opry*.

The story seems too good to be true—as if Hay had deliberately scouted central Tennessee for an aged fiddler with colorful stories to be a figurehead for the new show. But just then Thompson was in the news, having declared himself the nation's champion barn-dance fiddler and drawn the attention of rivals like Mellie Dunham in Maine. This also won him a session with Columbia, but the record didn't sell notably well, and in the fiddling contests that were rather a craze in 1925–26, like a sort of *America's Got Fiddling Talent*, Thompson made an early exit. He made one more record, a delightful interview with passages of fiddling, and died the following year, aged . . . well, less than he had claimed. During the contests, he (or a publicist) gave out that he was eighty-two—impressively older than merely septuagenarian competitors like Dunham. That would also have made him one of the oldest fiddlers on phonograph records. The fiction entered the *Opry* story and is perpetuated on his grave marker with a birth year of 1848. In fact, public records show he was born in 1854, and in the list of the oldest fiddlers to record, he barely makes the top ten.

Uncle Jimmy with his niece and piano accompanist, Eva Thompson Jones. Ms. Jones was also a trained contralto. For many years, she ran a Studio of Music and Dance on Nashville's Church Street.

Dates: b. May 25, 1875;
d. June 12, 1936; both Castalian Springs, TN
Instruments: harmonica, vocals
Recording Debut: March 3, 1928

KEY RECORDINGS

How Many Biscuits Can You Eat, **1928**
Goin' Up-Town, **1928**
Dill Pickle Rag, **1928**
Take Your Foot Out of the Mud and Put It in the Sand, **1928**
Old Joe, **1928**

WSM was not the first Nashville radio station to broadcast old-time music, though it was a close thing. The station came on air on October 5, 1925, but three weeks earlier, a more modest enterprise had made its debut, with the call letters WDAD, sponsored by Dad's auto and radio accessories store, and on September 24, it presented a segment by Dr. Humphrey Bate of Castalian Springs, northeast of Nashville, and his band. No doubt it would have sounded much like the organization that, two and a half years later, made records as Dr. Humphrey Bate and His Possum Hunters, playing fiddle tunes like "Billy in the Low Ground" alongside comic novelties a decade or two old like "My Wife Died Saturday Night" ("*and Tuesday I got married*").

With their rustic vocal refrains, fiddling, and banjo picking, these twelve recordings might seem to be standard-issue old-time stringband music, but as well as being enormously high spirited, they are made singular and delightful by the leader's sprightly harmonica playing. Though he chose to play on only half of the records, Dr. Bate was a very fine exponent of the "French harp," and he knew scores of tunes—a list he wrote out has survived, and it runs to 125. According to his daughter Alcyone, he had learned the majority of them from an elderly Black man.

In 1926, WDAD relocated and changed its call letters to WLAC. Bate then became a WSM stalwart, playing regularly on the *Opry* for several years, and went out on the road with WSM tours, Alcyone often playing piano for him. A group called the Possum Hunters, descended from the original, remained on the *Opry* until the mid-'60s before merging with the Crook Brothers, another harmonica-featuring band that had also been on the show since the 1920s.

The Possum Hunters, ca. 1928. *Standing*: Dr Bate, Jimmy Hart (guitar), Oscar Albright (bass). *Seated*: Staley Walton (guitar), Oscar Stone (fiddle), Walter Ligget (banjo).

SMITH'S SACRED SINGERS

Instruments: vocals, fiddle, piano, guitar
Recording Debut: April 23, 1926

KEY RECORDINGS

Pictures from Life's Other Side, **1926, 1934**
Where We'll Never Grow Old, **1926, 1934**
He Will Set Your Fields on Fire, **1927**
Let the Lower Lights Be Burning, **1928, 1934**
When They Ring the Golden Bells, **1934**

To the men creating the first record catalogs of old-time music, and to many of the performers who were contributing to them, gospel singing was a natural fit. **Uncle Dave Macon** could switch effortlessly from secular to sacred, from "Old Dan Tucker" to "Old Ship of Zion"; so could **Ernest Stoneman, the Carter Family**, and many other artists. The venerable tradition of quartet singing had been featured on discs since the early days, but in 1926 the nation's phonographs began to spin the less polished, more informal sounds of the Southern small-church quartet. The breakthrough was headed by a group from Braselton, Georgia, whose recent broadcast on WSB Atlanta had caught the ear of a Columbia Records talent scout. They were called Smith's Sacred Singers, and their debut single, "Pictures from Life's Other Side"/"Where We'll Never Grow Old," sold over 277,000 copies—the second-best-selling in Columbia's entire old-time list.

J. Frank Smith (1884–1937), a barber, singer, and singing-school teacher, was the group's leader and only fixture. The initial lineup of Clarence Cronic (tenor), Clyde Smith (baritone), and Marion L. Thrasher (bass) lasted a year or so. Then Thrasher (1885–1953), a minister, returned to his home state of Alabama and formed his own recording group, while Smith's move to Lawrenceville, Georgia, in 1927, occasioned a further change of personnel. Over the years there were shifts in the accompanying music too, deploying combinations of fiddle, guitar, and piano. In the course of a dozen recording sessions, at least ten men and women contributed to the group's extraordinary success. But the Singers' essential appeal was unimpaired, and in their nine-year career they not only dispensed favorite sacred songs to an avid audience on around three-quarters of a million discs but lit a path to the recording studio for many other Southern quartets.

Columbia *"New Process"* Records
REG. U. S. PAT. OFF.

SMITH'S SACRED SINGERS

SMITH'S SACRED SINGERS

J. FRANK SMITH, the leader of this group of inspired sacred singers, is widely known in the Southern States for his courageous work among the masses. Smith's Sacred Singers travel, by car, to every section of the South where they feel that good can be done. By them the word of God is taught in song. A preacher, capable of delivering a sermon, or, when necessary, doing his share of the singing, always goes on these trips.

Titles	Record No.
ARE YOU WASHED IN THE BLOOD OF THE LAMB JESUS DIED FOR ME—Vocals—Violin and Piano Accomps.	15430-D
MEET ME THERE—Guitar Accomp. WORKING FOR THE CROWN—Vocals—Violin and Piano Accomp.	15401-D
WHEN THE HAPPY MORNING BREAKS—Violin and Piano Accomp. I AM GOING THAT WAY—Vocals—Piano Accomp.	15389-D
LORD I'M COMING HOME WHEN JESUS COMES—Vocals	15371-D
THE UNCLOUDED DAY KEEP ON CLIMBING—Vocals	15351-D

MADE THE NEW WAY—ELECTRICALLY

[40]

The lineup of Smith's Sacred Singers had changed radically since their 1926 debut, but as late as 1929, Columbia was still using a photograph of the original group. J. Frank Smith stands far right.

FRANK HUTCHISON

Dates: b. March 20, 1897, Raleigh County, WV; d. November 9, 1945, Dayton, OH
Instruments: guitar, harmonica, vocals
Recording Debut: September 28, 1926

KEY RECORDINGS

Worried Blues, **1926, 1927**
(The) Train That Carried the Girl from Town, **1926, 1927**
Coney Isle, **1927**
The Last Scene of the Titanic, **1927**
The Miner's Blues, **1928**
Cannon Ball Blues, **1929**
K. C. Blues, **1929**

"Frank always specialized in the blues," said an associate, and his recordings are full of them: "Worried Blues," "Logan County Blues," "The Miner's Blues," "Cannon Ball Blues," "K. C. Blues." In fact, the names are sometimes deceptive: "Logan County Blues" is an old show-off guitar piece called "Spanish Fandango," while "K. C. Blues" is an instrumental version of the blues ballad "John Henry." But whatever the contours of the tune, Hutchison negotiates them with the skills and sensibility of a bluesman. He's supposed to have learned to play slide guitar from an African American guitarist and fellow Logan Countian, Bill Hunt. But he could fingerpick too, as on "Coney Isle" or "Cumberland Gap," or turn himself into a harmonica/guitar one-man band, as he did on "Stackalee," picked up many years later by Bob Dylan, or when playing old dance tunes like "The Wild Horse."

Logan County, West Virginia, where he lived, was deep coal country. Coal mining was hard work, and mining communities were tough audiences, but Hutchison, a miner himself, was a confident, versatile performer, proudly billing himself as "The Mountain State Record Maker (The Only West Virginian to Record Records of His Own Composition)." Yet, his disc career lasted for less than three years. In the fall of 1929, he participated in a phonographic oddity: a six-part impression of a medicine show that put him in the studio alongside **Fiddlin' John Carson** and other stars of Okeh Records. He comes across with great vitality, whamming on his guitar and telling jokes, and lives up to the billing the MC gives him of "The Pride of West Virginia"—but he never entered a recording studio again. He's said to have entertained on Ohio River steamers, and then to have given up music to run a store.

Above, Frank Hutchison as he appeared in Okeh's "Old Time Tunes" catalog, ca. 1927–28. *Right*, a portrait of the artist as a young man, his cowboy-outfit wooly chaps resembling those worn by cowboys for warmth (and to repel rain or snow) in cold regions.

McFARLAND & GARDNER ("MAC & BOB")

Dates: Lester McFarland, b. February 2, 1902; d. July 24, 1984. Robert A. Gardner, b. December 16, 1897; d. September 30, 1978; all Oliver Springs, TN
Instruments: mandolin, guitar, harmonica, vocals
Recording Debut: October 13, 1926

KEY RECORDINGS

When the Roses Bloom Again, **1926**
Three Leaves of Shamrock, **1927**
Where the River Shannon Flows, **1927**
There's No One Like Mother to Me, **1929**
When It's Lamp Lightin' Time in the Valley, **1933**

We often say "Nashville" to mean the symbolic home of country music. But what if the music's origin story had begun somewhere else? Say, 180 miles east across Tennessee, in the city of *Knox*ville? It could so easily have happened. Knoxville is accessible to half a dozen states, a confluence of the great rivers of Appalachian song. In the 1920s, it staged fiddling contests and boasted talented local artists like the one-man bands George Reneau and Charlie Oaks, or the graceful singer Hugh Cross.

More successful than any of these were a couple of songsters billed, rather formally, under their names of Lester McFarland and Robert A. Gardner, later shortened to "Mac & Bob." They owned a vast compendium of old-time balladry and Victorian parlor song, which they presented in close harmony, prettily accompanied on mandolin, guitar, and harmonica. Compared with **Fiddlin' John Carson** or **Charlie Poole**, they sounded a little straitlaced, but they endeared themselves to listeners who sought story more than style with their earnest tales of parted lovers and remembered mothers—all the pressed flowers in the Victorian songbook. Over six years, they stocked the Vocalion and Brunswick catalogs with almost two hundred recordings, many of them also issued in Australia and the UK.

McFarland was blind, Gardner partially sighted, and they may have met in blind school. For several years they were based in Knoxville, but in the '30s they sang to the huge radio audience of WLS in Chicago. **Bill Monroe** heard them there and would acknowledge their influence on his and his brother Charlie's duets for mandolin and guitar. After they retired, they stayed on in Chicago, doing good works among the city's disadvantaged.

"Mac and Bob" promoted themselves not only through their many recordings on Vocalion (*above left*) and its sister label Brunswick, but with theater tours that took them as far west as Texas. *Above right*: This songbook was published in 1931, by which time Mac & Bob had left Tennessee for Chicago, where they were heard regularly on radio station WLS.

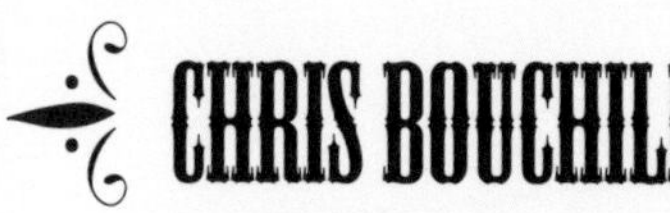

CHRIS BOUCHILLON

Dates: Christophe Allen Bouchillon,
b. August 21, 1893, Anderson County, SC;
d. September 18, 1968, West Palm Beach, FL
Instrument: vocal
Recording Debut: ca. July 7, 1925 [with the Bouchillon Trio]

KEY RECORDINGS

Talking Blues, **1926**
Born in Hard Luck, **1927**
The Medicine Show, **1927**
Speed Maniac, **1928**
Girls of Today, **1928**

"Here It Is—Columbia's Newest Hit by It's [*sic*] Newest Musician," ran the headline over a full-page ad for old-time records. It was February 1927, and the record was Chris Bouchillon's "Talking Blues." It sold over ninety thousand copies and created a new category of music.

Bouchillon (the name was of French Huguenot origin) was from Greenville, South Carolina, where he worked as a machinist. In his time off, he sang and played ukulele with his younger brothers, Charley on fiddle and John Urias on guitar. A report of a "musical entertainment and box supper" called them "well-known foot warmers of this section."

What Bouchillon (or Columbia) titled "Talking Blues" was a series of verses, delivered as if through the smoke of a corncob pipe, over Urias's ragtime or blues lines. "*It ain't no use me a-workin' so hard—I got a woman in the white folks' yard*" gives you the flavor. Its subjects, and those of 1928's "New Talking Blues," were idleness, chicken stealing, chitlins—supposedly comic images of supposed African American life and behavior, century-old tropes of the blackface minstrel stage. Other artists copied these routines, sometimes with racial epithets in the titles to make clear who was being made fun of. Bouchillon, however, soon redirected his armchair commentaries toward nonracial topics like unruly flappers and scolding wives. In "The Medicine Show," he gives instructions for use: "*Shake bottle well before using. Shake husband well after using.*" "Born in Hard Luck" opens "*I was born on the last month in the year,*" and progresses to "*the last second in the minute . . . to tell the truth about it, I like not to got here at all.*" Hillbilly artists continued to recycle or revise the talking blues, to be joined by Woody Guthrie and, after him, Bob Dylan.

CHRIS BOUCHILLON

"The Talking Comedian of the South"

WHEN Chris Bouchillon says anything he does it in such a dry, humorous sort of way that you can't help but laugh.

Chris isn't averse to a bit of playing and singing, now and then, either. When he tunes up his voice and guitar, folks come from miles around to hear the melodies of this popular South Carolina minstrel.

In addition to being one of the foremost wits and singers of the South, Chris can tinker with an auto just as effectively as with a tune.

CHRIS BOUCHILLON

"So . . . *I got me another job, in a ladies' shoe store. All I had to do, when a lady came in to try on a pair of shoes, was just to lace up her laces. But the boss fired me there. He said I got above my job. . . . Oh, I'm in hard luck, ain't no doubt of that.*" From "Born in Hard Luck" (right).

BURNETT & RUTHERFORD

Dates: Richard Daniel Burnett, b. October 8, 1883, Wayne County, KY; d. January 23, 1977, Somerset, KY
Leonard Rutherford, b. March 22, 1898; d. June 30, 1951; both Somerset, KY
Instruments: fiddle, banjo, guitar, vocals
Recording Debut: November 6, 1926

KEY RECORDINGS

Little Stream of Whiskey, **1926**
A Short Life of Trouble, **1926**
Willie Moore, **1927**
Ladies on the Steamboat, **1927**
Cumberland Gap, **1928**

Dick Burnett boasted that he and Leonard Rutherford "played every note exactly together." Frank Walker, who supervised their Columbia recordings, acknowledged that they were wonderfully smooth, and added, as Burnett recalled, "You have some of the tantalizingest names for these records that ever I listened at." Yet, his admiration didn't extend to paying royalties, even though their records sold very well, and the musicians, piqued, took themselves off to Gennett for a while.

Burnett played music all his life: dulcimer and harmonica as a child, then banjo, guitar, and fiddle. Blinded in a robbery at twenty-four, he parlayed his skills into a career as a traveling musician, covering southern Kentucky and getting as far north as Cincinnati. Rutherford, who had been orphaned in his twenties, joined him, and Burnett taught him all he knew about music. Showmanship, however, was beyond the younger man; as his mentor remarked, there was "no monkey work about him at all." But the music they made was marvelous, the delicacy of Rutherford's fiddling in perfect concord with Burnett's vocal phrasing. The two men played together for thirty-five years, until their partnership was ended by Rutherford's early death from epilepsy.

When on the road, Burnett sold not only their own and other people's records but also ten-cent songbooks that he had printed; he told historian Charles Wolfe that he had dispensed six thousand of them. One of the pieces, titled "Farewell Song," is an early text of "I Am a Man of Constant Sorrow," since made famous in the movie *O Brother, Where Art Thou?* Burnett never recorded it, and it was left to a Wayne County acquaintance, the singer and guitarist Emry Arthur, to put it on disc for the first time in 1928. Whether Burnett composed this incomparable existential lament, we may never know.

The Southern Kentucky Mountaineers who played "Cumberland Gap" were Rutherford, Burnett (*left* and *right*, respectively, in above photo), and guitarist Byrd Moore. Originally from Virginia, Moore was then working as a barber in eastern Tennessee. He also played guitar on records by Clarence "Tom" Ashley, Earl Johnson, and others.

GEORGIA YELLOW HAMMERS

Instruments: fiddle, banjo, guitars, ukulele, vocals
Recording Debut: February 18, 1927

KEY RECORDINGS

Fourth of July at a Country Fair, **1927**
The Picture on the Wall, **1927**
I'm S-A-V-E-D, **1927**
How I Got My Wife [as Bill Chitwood & His Georgia Mountaineers], **1927**
G Rag, **1927**
All Gone Now [as the Clyde Evans Band], **1929**

The runaway success of **the Skillet-Lickers** in 1926 galvanized rival record companies to discover stringbands equally potent and versatile. Within months, the Georgia Yellow Hammers emerged from Gordon County in northwestern Georgia. The band's core was banjoist Bud Landress (1882–1966) and fiddler Bill Chitwood (1888–1961), who had already made records, augmented by Ernest Moody (1891–1977) on ukulele, and guitarists Phil Reeve (1897–1949) and Clyde Evans (1906–74). Few bands were so variously gifted. Chitwood (and Landress) could wield a strong, bluesy fiddle, and Landress was an imaginative songwriter. All had a background in sacred singing. They could turn from breakdowns to comic novelties, and their ingenious arrangements of old-time songs with vocal quartet settings were imitated by other groups elsewhere. Their Victor record of "Picture on the Wall" and "My Carolina Girl" was a six-figure seller in 1927–28. Moody, a respected writer of hymns, said that he earned more money from that than from any of his other work.

The Yellow Hammers were the nucleus of much music making in their area, recombining with other musicians to make records, for several labels, of yodel songs, blues, shape-note singing, and humorous sketches, along with imperishable comic numbers like "Fourth of July at a Country Fair" and "Song of the Doodle Bug." Landress and Chitwood staged fiddlers' conventions and all-day singings, while Reeve directed a brass band for picnics and evening entertainments. He also procured a recording deal for two local African American musicians, fiddler Andrew Baxter (1874–1955) and his guitarist son Jim (1898–1950), who thus preserved a Black tradition that phonograph records only scantily documented. Exceptionally, for the period, Andrew Baxter plays *with* the Yellow Hammers on their record of "G Rag."

Gordon County's finest, ca. 1927. *Standing*: C. E. Moody, Phil Reeve. *Seated*: Bud Landress, Bill Chitwood. Reeve worked at a music store in Calhoun, Georgia, and with his inside knowledge of the recording business was able to promote the band to Victor producer Ralph S. Peer.

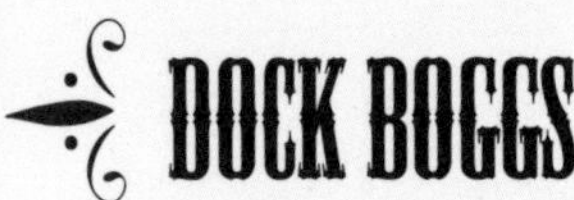

DOCK BOGGS

Dates: Moran Lee ("Dock" or "Doc") Boggs, b. February 7, 1898, Wise County, VA; d. February 7, 1971, Norton, VA
Instruments: banjo, vocals
Recording Debut: March 10, 1927

KEY RECORDINGS

Country Blues, **1927**
Down South Blues, **1927**
Pretty Polly, **1927**
False Hearted Lover's Blues, **1929**
Old Rub Alcohol Blues, **1929**

Dock Boggs was a singer and banjo player who made a handful of records in the late 1920s, gigged for a while around the coalfields, and then resumed his life as a coal miner. Haled out of retirement by Mike Seeger in the '60s, he performed for the first time for urban audiences at Newport and other folk festivals and aired his considerable repertoire on three LPs. Yet, despite these exposures, he is a hard man to get a clear view of. Recent scholars have envisioned him as a deep, strange figure whose music reaches us from an "old weird America."

Some caution is necessary here. What seems weird in academia may be everyday in Appalachia. Dock Boggs needs no existential trappings; he is fascinating enough in his own right. He certainly impressed William E. Myer, an entrepreneur from Richlands, Virginia, who, after hearing his first recordings for Brunswick, wrote a batch of songs for Boggs and even created a record label, Lonesome Ace, to issue them. Compositions such as "Old Rub Alcohol Blues" and "Will Sweethearts Know Each Other There" suggest that Myer appreciated some of the complexities of Boggs's musical imagination.

Like many of his contemporaries, Boggs had had a road-to-Damascus moment when he first heard a Black musician, but, more than most, he seems to have let African American music saturate his own, shading everything blue. "Down South Blues" draws most of its text from a record by the Black singer Clara Smith, but "Country Blues"—not in the blues form—is an amalgamation of old-time musical structure and Black sensibility, a bridge connecting the ancient broadside "Come all ye," via the blues, to the confessional narrative of honky-tonk. This is neither old nor weird; indeed, you could just as well argue that it is a lightning-strike moment of modernism.

"Dock" Boggs, pictured around the time he made his first recordings in New York in March 1927. He had been selected by Brunswick Records from several dozen hopefuls at a talent contest in Norton, Virginia.

DEFORD BAILEY

Dates: b. December 14, 1899, Smith County, TN;
d. July 2, 1982, Nashville, TN
Instrument: harmonica, guitar, banjo, vocals
Recording Debut: April 1, 1927

KEY RECORDINGS

Pan American Blues, **1927**
Evening Prayer Blues, **1927**
Fox Chase, **1927**
John Henry, **1928**
Davidson County Blues, **1928**

In the 1920s and '30s, DeFord Bailey was probably the nation's best-known African American "folk" musician. For fifteen years, he played harmonica on the *Grand Ole Opry*, a show he would often introduce, as he had in its earliest days, with his impression of a train, the "Pan American Blues." In 1927–28, he recorded it, along with other imitations of trains and fox chases, and several blues. He was popular with fellow *Opry* musicians like **Dr. Humphrey Bate**, who introduced him to WSM, and **Bill Monroe**, who played Bailey's tune "Evening Prayer Blues" over his grave. Nevertheless, in 1941, for complicated reasons to do with music copyright, the show's management decided to discard him and his now somewhat old-fashioned music. He left the public stage entirely and operated a shoeshine stand on Nashville's 12th Avenue. Three decades later, a new generation of old-time music fans began taking an interest in him, discovering that as well as a superb harmonica player he was also an original guitarist and banjoist—a side of him seldom seen in his *Opry* days but revealed by the album *The Legendary DeFord Bailey*.

Though his association with the *Opry* has made him stand out as a Black musician on an otherwise white hillbilly show, Bailey was not unique. At the same time, in the Midwest, a Texas-born African American named Freeman Stowers, a.k.a. "Checkerboard Sam," was playing train tunes on the harmonica and doing farmyard impressions, on radio, records, and wide-ranging personal appearances, sponsored by the animal-feed manufacturer Purina. Like Bailey, who had suffered polio in childhood, he was small in stature, and one suspects that these men's access to the public on white programs was possible only because they were regarded as unthreatening oddities and so were treated less as colleagues than as mascots.

DeFord Bailey on the stage of the *Grand Ole Opry*. The adapted megaphone increased the volume and resonance of his harmonica.

BUELL KAZEE

Dates: Buell Hilton Kazee, b. August 29, 1900, Magoffin County, KY; d. August 31, 1976, Winchester, KY
Instruments: banjo, guitar, vocals
Recording Debut: April 19, 1927

KEY RECORDINGS

John Hardy, **1927**
Darling Cora, **1927**
East Virginia, **1927**
The Little Mohee, **1927**
The Butcher's Boy, **1928**
The Wagoner's Lad, **1928**
Steel a Goin' Down, **1929**

Buell Kazee was a man of two worlds. As an interpreter of old ballads, he stood both within and outside his culture, singing and playing them with authentic skill and expressiveness—"I grew up with the old, the genuine thing," he said; "I can almost go back to the original"—yet he was as conscious of their long history and complex meanings as any academic folklorist. Like many other Kentucky musicians, he played rippling, intricate tunes on the banjo, but atypically he had taken voice training, and the contrast between his grave, formal singing and the vivacious accenting of its accompaniment is unparalleled in old-time music.

He became a recording artist by happenstance. A casual remark to the owner of his local music store that he knew some old songs led to a call from Brunswick Records, and within weeks he was in New York to begin recording what would become a remarkable catalog of old (sometimes Old World) ballads and mountain folk songs: "John Hardy," "Darling Cora," "East Virginia," "The Butcher's Boy," "Lady Gay," "The Wagoner's Lad," and many more. But he was no purist; he sang cowboy songs and pop songs and even participated in a couple of comic sketches, "A Mountain Boy Makes His First Record" and "Election Day in Kentucky." Perhaps because his singing was so clear, some of his records were released in the UK, Ireland, and Australia.

His disc career lasted only a couple of years—a brief distraction from his life's work in the Baptist ministry. "My entire time is spent," he said, "in preaching and teaching the Bible, holding meetings and Bible conferences, and pastoring a church." But he gave occasional recitals of mountain songs, and, after Joan Baez recorded his versions of "East Virginia" and "Wagoner's Lad," he appeared at the Newport Folk Festival.

Buell Kazee in 1973 (and, in the picture on the wall, 1927). "Darling Cora" has become a bluegrass standard.

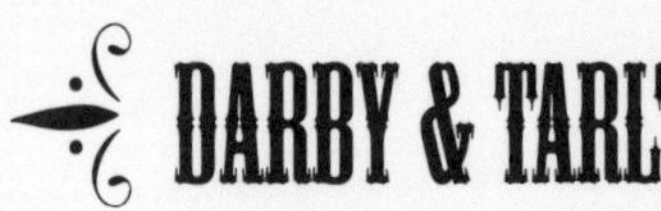

DARBY & TARLTON

Dates: Tom Darby, b. August 25, 1891; d. August 20, 1971; both Columbus, GA
John James Rimbert (Jimmie) Tarlton, b. May 8, 1892, Cheraw, SC; d. November 29, 1979, Phenix City, AL
Instruments: steel guitar, guitar, vocals
Recording Debut: April 5, 1927

KEY RECORDINGS

Birmingham Jail, **1927**
Columbus Stockade Blues, **1927**
Sweet Sarah Blues, **1929**
Frankie Dean, **1930**
Lowe Bonnie, **1930**

"Hawaiian music will become a fad," an Iowa newspaper predicted in 1898, "for the native songs are plaintive and weird." A craze for Hawaiian music did sweep the nation over the next couple of decades—especially for Hawaiian guitar playing, whose swoops, slides, and shimmers evoked dreams of moonlight and mystery. Many young guitarists learned to play that way from tutor books or touring Hawaiian acts but, feeling the pull of their own familial and regional traditions, adapted the Hawaiian method to the old-time repertoire of ballads, parlor songs, comic pieces, and, above all, blues.

One of the first old-time acts to exploit this transition from the South Sea Islands to the Southern highlands was Darby & Tarlton. On their second record, "Columbus Stockade Blues" and "Birmingham Jail," their rugged harmony and Tarlton's slide guitar runs gave a new character to two well-loved old songs. The disc sold almost two hundred thousand copies, and thereafter the duo basked in the warm regard of Columbia Records—all the warmer, perhaps, because Darby insisted they were paid a flat fee for their recordings rather than (as it would have proved) more lucrative royalties. And they were wonderful recordings, the honeyed sweetness of Tarlton's voice a perfect foil for Darby's craggier manner, Tarlton's slide guitar coruscating in pieces like "Sweet Sarah Blues" or his solo "Lowe Bonnie," based on the Old World ballad "Lord Randal."

After their Columbia contract ended, they made a few records for Victor and ARC, but they were among the many craftspeople of old-time music who would be shouldered aside by younger and more assertive musicians working at the faster tempo of what was coming to be called "rural rhythm." Tarlton briefly returned in the '60s to make a few festival appearances and an estimable album. He was still sore about the royalties.

Even as record buying slackened during 1929–30, following the Wall Street Crash of October 1929, Columbia could rely on Darby and Tarlton to rack up sales on a par with Riley Puckett and the Skillet-Lickers.

THE ALLEN BROTHERS

Dates: Austin Ambrose Allen, b. February 7, 1901, Sewanee, TN; d. January 5, 1959, Williamston, SC
Lee William Allen, b. June 1, 1906, Sewanee, TN; d. February 24, 1981, Lebanon, TN
Instruments: banjo, guitar, kazoo, vocals
Recording Debut: April 7, 1927

KEY RECORDINGS

Salty Dog, **1927–34**
Tiple Blues, **1928**
I've Got the Chain Store Blues, **1930**
Jake Walk Blues, **1930**
(Hey Buddy, Won't You) Roll Down the Line, **1930, 1934**

Though the idiom they worked in was called old-time, many of the Allen Brothers' songs were modern, dealing with issues that mattered to Southerners during the Depression. Among their subjects were Prohibition ("The Enforcement Blues," "Fruit Jar Blues"), the economics of farming ("Price of Cotton Blues"), and the antagonism between small stores and the big chains ("I've Got the Chain Store Blues"). The disconcertingly jokey "Jake Walk Blues" described the early '30s epidemic of "jakeitis," a paralytic condition caused by the unprohibited alcoholic beverage Jamaica Ginger, after a batch was distributed that had been adulterated with a neurotoxin.

These topical songs, like much of the rest of their output, were written as blues, which, Lee Allen later attested, were popular with white folk in their part of the country; the brothers were based in Chattanooga, Tennessee. The Allens gave them lively accompaniments on banjo (Austin) and guitar (Lee), with Lee inserting snorting mock-trumpet breaks on kazoo. In up-tempo numbers such as their bestselling "A New Salty Dog," they swung like a jugless jug band. How close their music was to Black models may be judged by the fact that one of their records, "Chattanooga Blues" coupled with "Laughin' and Cryin' Blues," was released in Columbia's "race" catalog and advertised in the African American press.

That may have been why the Allens quickly deserted Columbia for Victor, where producer Ralph Peer encouraged their songwriting and recorded them at regular intervals; over four years they made some fifty recordings, several with suggestive lyrics, as in "Pile Drivin' Papa," "Warm Knees Blues," or "Shake It, Ida, Shake It." After a couple of years' break, they returned in 1934 for a final session, now for Vocalion, celebrating Franklin D. Roosevelt's National Recovery Administration in "New Deal Blues" and reprising the ever-popular "Salty Dog."

Singing

10-inch, List Price 75c

23662 I'll Be Here a Long, Long Time
It Can't Be Done
with Guitar and Kazoo
Allen Brothers

ALLEN BROTHERS

23664 Gene, the Fighting Marine
Bobby Boy
with Orchestra
Graham Brothers

23668 Hard Times Come No More
Spring's Tornado
with Piano
Graham Brothers

Eleven Months and Ten Days More—Part 3
with Pipe Organ
Jim Baird
Don't Hang Me in the Morning
with Violin, Guitar and Piano
Graham Brothers
No. 23670

She's Just That Kind—No. 2
First Time in Jail
with Guitar, Kazoo and Harmonica
Fleming and Townsend
No. 23666

RCA Victor Company, Inc., Camden, N. J.

A Radio Corporation of America Subsidiary

Promotional flyer for new Victor releases, 1932. The cartoon figures could have come straight out of a humorous magazine of the period like the *New Yorker*. The Allen Brothers' recording "I'll Be Here a Long, Long Time" borrowed the tune of the recent blues hit "Sitting on Top of the World."

DACOSTA WOLTZ'S SOUTHERN BROADCASTERS

Instruments: fiddle, banjos, vocals
Recording Debut: May 5, 1927

KEY RECORDINGS

Yellow Rose of Texas, **1927**
Richmond Cotillion, **1927**
Are You Washed in the Blood of the Lamb, **1927**
Take Me Back to the Sweet Sunny South, **1927**
Jack of Diamonds, **1927**

Old-time band names don't get much more exotic than this, which may be one reason why enthusiasts regard this group with awe, but chiefly it's because Mr. Woltz's ambitiously titled crew made such extraordinary music. The core members, originating in Surry County, North Carolina, were fiddler Ben Jarrell (1880–1946), banjoist and fiddler Frank Jenkins (1888–1945), and their banjo-playing leader (1892–1941). They also boasted a special attraction: the teenaged Price Goodson, who sang and played harmonica and ukulele. But there was no guitarist. Untethered by a rhythm setter at the low end of the sonic spectrum, the twin banjoists weaved intricately around each other, achieving a wild freedom unmatched in recorded old-time music.

Woltz, sometime mayor of Galax, Virginia, was probably the band's moving spirit and the one who named them. Historians have wondered if "Broadcasters" was an invented PR claim, but the band did play at least one prestigious radio gig. After completing their session at Gennett Records' studio in Richmond, Indiana, they stopped off on the way home in Cincinnati, where Gennett had arranged a promotional broadcast to illustrate "the music of the genuine old-time fiddlers' conventions."

In their three days in Indiana, the group made sixteen recordings. A few, such as "Richmond Cotillion" and the sacred pieces "Are You Washed in the Blood of the Lamb" and "I Know My Name Is There," sold widely on cut-price labels, but Gennett never called back. In 1929, Frank Jenkins and his son Oscar cut some powerful sides with **Ernest Stoneman**, like "The Burial of Wild Bill." But that was not the end of it: The legacy was borne far into the twentieth century by Oscar Jenkins and especially by fiddler and banjoist Tommy Jarrell, Ben's son, a pillar of the local musical community and teacher of countless younger players.

From left: Frank Jenkins, Price Goodson, Ben Jarrell, DaCosta Woltz. When their recordings were issued on budget labels like Challenge, the Southern Broadcasters acquired a new name, becoming Frank Neal and His Boys.

TAYLOR'S KENTUCKY BOYS

Instruments: fiddle, banjo, guitar, vocals
Recording Debut: April 26, 1927

KEY RECORDINGS

Gray Eagle, **1927**
Forked Deer, **1927**
Soldier['s] Joy, **1927**
Maxwell Girl, **1927**
Coal Creek March [Marion Underwood banjo solo], **1927**
Sourwood Mountain, **1927**

The old-time fiddlers' contest was an arena generally closed to African American musicians (except for all-Black affairs, of which several are documented in the early twentieth century). Yet, to conclude from this that old-time fiddling has no African American components in its makeup would be to seriously misunderstand its history. We know Black fiddlers were active throughout the nineteenth century, playing what we now call old-time tunes and often teaching them to their white neighbors. But in the twentieth century, this role was obscured—in part by the recording industry, which treated almost all Black musicians as blues or jazz players and paid little attention to what was still, as late as the 1920s, a living heritage of Black fiddling and stringband music, connected to and intriguingly different from the music of white contemporaries.

Among the few recordings that slipped through this filter are those of the African American fiddler Jim Booker (1872–1940) of Jessamine County, Kentucky, who headed a recording band organized by a local white entrepreneur, Dennis W. Taylor, and billed as Taylor's Kentucky Boys. The other members, such as banjoist Marion Underwood (1882–1939) and singer/guitarist Aulton Ray (1909–82), were white. Performances like "Gray Eagle" and "Forked Deer" are graced with old-time fiddling of extraordinary verve, justifying the respect in which Booker was held by white neighbors like fiddler Doc Roberts, another of Taylor's stable of recording musicians. On a few sides made later the same year, such as "Sourwood Mountain," Roberts (and sometimes Underwood) joins Booker's own family stringband. Such racial mixing in the recording studio was then exceedingly rare, and the brilliance of the music it produced is a poignant testimony to how much has been lost in the near obliteration from the historical record of African American fiddling and stringband traditions.

Gennetts of Old Time Tunes

Taylor's Kentucky Boys

TAYLOR'S KENTUCKY BOYS

FORKED DEER—*Old Time Playin'*	6130
GRAY EAGLE—*Old Time Playin'*	.75

An image of concealment. Banjoist Marion Underwood and guitarist Aulton Ray, being white, could be portrayed in Gennett's catalog of "Old Time Tunes," but fiddler Jim Booker, being Black, could not. For the photograph, his place was taken by the band's manager and nominal leader, Dennis W. Taylor.

BLIND ALFRED REED

Dates: b. June 17, 1880, Floyd, VA; d. January 17, 1956, Shady Springs, WV
Instruments: fiddle, vocals
Recording Debut: July 28, 1927

KEY RECORDINGS

The Wreck of the Virginian, **1927**

Why Do You Bob Your Hair, Girls, **1927**

Woman's Been After Man Ever Since, **1929**

How Can a Poor Man Stand Such Times and Live, **1929**

Black and Blue Blues, **1929**

How could an American woman of the 1920s declare herself (in a popular phrase of the time) "free, white, and twenty-one"? By bobbing her hair. In doing so, she not only rejected a core image of womanliness as understood by earlier generations but sowed the mischievous seeds of gender uncertainty. Add her short skirts and bold makeup, and this New Woman became a sore affliction to older or more conventional folks. Such people might have found a standard-bearer in the fiddling evangelist of Mercer County, West Virginia, who sang, "*Why do you bob your hair, girls? You're doing mighty wrong. God says it is a glory, and you should wear it long*." The song spread widely enough that its maker was called two years later to record a follow-up and took the opportunity to issue further diatribes all about Eve: "Woman's Been After Man Ever Since," "Black and Blue Blues," and the resigned "We've Got to Have 'Em, That's All."

We may wonder how seriously we should take Blind Alfred Reed in these solemn but never-quite-humorless sermons against modernity, with their sometimes almost jaunty accompaniments on fiddle and guitar. But no one doubts the gravity of what has become, thanks in part to Ry Cooder and Bruce Springsteen, Reed's best-remembered song. In "How Can a Poor Man Stand Such Times and Live," recorded mere weeks after the Wall Street Crash, he rounds up the underclass's usual suspects: cheating store owners, duplicitous doctors, hypocritical ministers. (Add bankers and politicians, and you might be listening to Woody Guthrie.) In his other songs, he exchanged the polemicist's pen for the journalist's, telling stories of local train wrecks or coal mine explosions. His legacy of fewer than twenty recordings may be small, but his messages echo resoundingly down the decades.

Blind Alfred Reed (*center*) with his son Orville on guitar and Fred Pendleton of Princeton, West Virginia, on fiddle. Traveling musicians often customized their vehicles with homemade advertisements. As well as accompanying Alfred Reed, Pendleton and Orville Reed made a few records as the West Virginia Night Owls.

JIMMIE RODGERS

Dates: James Charles Rodgers, b. September 8, 1897, Meridian, MS; d. May 26, 1933, New York, NY
Instruments: guitar, vocals
Recording Debut: August 4, 1927

KEY RECORDINGS

Blue Yodel, **1927**
The Brakeman's Blues, **1928**
In the Jailhouse Now, **1928**
Waiting for a Train, **1928**
Any Old Time, **1929**
My Rough and Rowdy Ways, **1929**
Jimmie the Kid, **1931**

You could tell Jimmie Rodgers's story in headlines: "Yodeling Ex-Railroader Scores Nationwide Hit" (1928), "Builds Texas Mansion, Calls It 'Blue Yodeler's Paradise'" (1930), "Succumbs to TB" (1933). In under six years, the lanky singer and guitarist from Mississippi conquered the nation with songs of rambling and gambling, fast trains and faster women, family and home, colored by his good-humored drawl and bluesy guitar figures and decorated with a yodel. His music was exported to Britain, Australia, and India. In Kenya, the Kipsigi people heard his records and thought him a god, "Chemirocha."

Rodgers is routinely called "The Father of Country Music." It's a description he might have acknowledged with a wry shrug. Certainly, his style has left indelible marks on the pages of country music's history, and no other artist's songs have been so copied. But when we look at how he shaped his career, we find him heading not down the dusty highways of hillbilly music but uptown, toward "*the lights of old Broadway*," where professional writers provided his songs and studio musicians played on them. Had he lived longer, he might have become a pop balladeer like his contemporary Gene Austin, a Southern counterpart to Bing Crosby or Rudy Vallee. Or perhaps not; it would have required some adjustments. His success was founded upon two words, the title of his first hit, "Blue Yodel." Play down the yodeling, wash away the blues, and what would be left? He died before the question could be answered.

That we can still speculate about Rodgers's unfulfilled future testifies to the unique fascination of the work he left us, which has drawn artists from Merle Haggard to Bob Dylan to recall and reconstruct it. No other figure from country music's first generation is so alive in the present.

Rodgers's signature guitar was made for him by Weymann & Son of Philadelphia, Pennsylvania, manufacturers of high-end guitars and banjos.

THE CARTER FAMILY

Instruments: guitars, autoharp, vocals
Recording Debut: August 1, 1927

KEY RECORDINGS

Single Girl, Married Girl, **1927**, **1935**
Keep on the Sunny Side, **1928**, **1935**
Will You Miss Me When I'm Gone?, **1928**, **1935**
Wildwood Flower, **1928**, **1935**
I'm Thinking Tonight of My Blue Eyes, **1929**, **1935**
Can the Circle Be Unbroken?, **1935**
Hello Stranger, **1937**

The Carters are the First Family of country music—in two senses. Three generations have contributed to the genre, but, more importantly, the original trio was the first singing group to become widely known through records and radio. They oversaw the transformation of old Southern song into a nationally marketed product.

Alvin Pleasant Carter (1891–1960) and Sara Dougherty Carter (1898–1979), who married in 1915, sang around southwestern Virginia, Sara playing autoharp or guitar. In 1926 they found, in A. P.'s sister-in-law Maybelle Addington Carter (1909–78), both a compatible third voice and a wonderful guitarist, and when Victor Records came to Bristol, Virginia, in the summer of 1927, the Carters were emboldened to audition. When producer Ralph Peer first heard Sara sing, he knew he had struck gold, and he guided their career, on Victor and other labels, for more than a decade. Their repertoire, drawn largely from A. P.'s field collecting, was sober and god-fearing, in contrast with the good-time blues of their contemporary **Jimmie Rodgers**, but the two acts were friendly—they even recorded some endearingly awkward comic sketches together. A. P. and Sara divorced in 1936, but the extended family continued to work together, on broadcasts from TexMex border radio stations that were heard across the nation.

In the '40s and '50s, A. P. and Sara maintained their working relationship, supported by their children, Janette and Joe, but it was Maybelle, now mainly playing autoharp, and her daughters, Helen, June, and Anita, who chiefly promoted the Carter name on records, radio, and the *Grand Ole Opry*. The original Family's election to the Country Music Hall of Fame in 1970 acknowledged that they possessed one of the most influential sounds in American music, reaching beyond old-time country to bluegrass, and, via Woody Guthrie, to Bob Dylan.

With its valuable portfolio of songs copyrighted by the Carter Family and Jimmie Rodgers, Ralph S. Peer's Southern Music became a major player in country music song publishing. *Left to right:* Maybelle, A. P., Sara.

LOWE STOKES

Dates: Marcus Lowell Stokes, b. May 28, 1898, Ellijay, GA; d. July 14, 1983, Chouteau, OK
Instruments: fiddle, organ, vocals
Recording Debut: October 31, 1927

KEY RECORDINGS

Take Me Back to Georgia, **1929**
Wish I Had Stayed in the Wagon Yard, **1929**
Sally Johnson, **1930**
Four Cent Cotton, **1930**
Citaco [with the Swamp Rooters], **1930**

Lowe Stokes never got his dues. Though he played on many records by the hugely popular **Skillet-Lickers**, he never received a label credit, and **Clayton McMichen**, when interviewed about the band, mentioned him only in passing. On his own recordings, he was sometimes oddly reticent, giving generous space to the singer or the astonishing teenage guitarist Hoke Rice. Yet, he had had an explosive entry onto the stage of old-time music, circa 1924, when he beat **Fiddlin' John Carson** in a big Atlanta fiddling contest. He proved to be one of the great fiddlers of his era, and on the four sides where he fiddles with just a guitarist, his playing twists like a rattlesnake. (As it happens, "Take Me Back to Georgia" is also known as "Rattlesnake Bit the Baby.") "Four Cent Cotton," "Somebody's Rocking My Sugar Lump," and "Citaco," with their tearaway twin fiddling, share the furious momentum of the Skillet-Lickers. But on a recording date, Stokes was just as likely to play some pop tune of his youth like "Sailing on the Robert E. Lee." Perhaps, like McMichen, he wanted to prove that he was not some straw-chewing hick but an up-to-the-minute musician—a professional.

Stokes didn't have much chance to develop that kind of a career. On Christmas Day 1930, he intervened in a fight, grabbed someone's pistol, and had most of his right hand—his bowing hand—shot off. He took a stiff drink of whiskey while a doctor performed a quick amputation, then went to a barbershop for a shave. Within a year or two he could fiddle again, using a prosthetic, and for two decades he played in obscurity, eventually retiring and settling in Oklahoma. In the last few years of his life, urged on by musician friends, he picked up the fiddle again.

Lowe Stokes at his home in Oklahoma, 1969. Over the next decade or so, he resumed playing again. One of his last public performances was at the 1982 Brandywine Festival of the Arts in Wilmington, Delaware, when he played "Hell Broke Loose in Georgia."

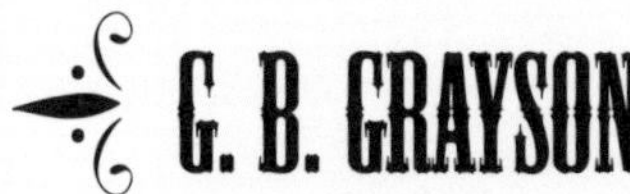

G. B. GRAYSON

Dates: Gilliam Banmon (or Bandman) Grayson,
b. November 11, 1887, possibly Laurel Bloomery, TN;
d. August 16, 1930, near Damascus, VA
Instruments: fiddle, vocals
Recording Debut: October 1927

KEY RECORDINGS

Handsome Molly, **1927**
Ommie Wise, **1927**
Train Forty-Five, **1927**
Short Life of Trouble, **1928**
Little Maggie with a Dram Glass in Her Hand, **1928**
Tom Dooley, **1929**

G. B. Grayson could play a dance tune or a comic novelty as well as any fiddler, but it isn't for pieces like "Cluck Old Hen" that he is revered; rather, it's for the stately seriousness of his singing in the murder ballads "Ommie Wise," "Rose Conley," and "Tom Dooley," or the stoic resignation of "Short Life of Trouble." Singing and fiddling at the same time always impressed listeners, but in Grayson's case there was more to it than that: the tonalities of voice and instrument echo and elide into each other, to powerful effect.

Partially sighted since early childhood, Grayson nonetheless traveled around North Carolina, Tennessee, and Virginia, playing for house parties, busking on the street, and occasionally entering a fiddling contest. At one such event in Mountain City, Tennessee, in 1927, he met **Henry Whitter**—a recording star a few years earlier, now looking for a partner whose talent might revive his own drooping career. With his inside knowledge of the record business, Whitter secured them sessions a few weeks apart with both Gennett and Victor. Their second Victor release, "Handsome Molly" and "Train Forty-Five," sold very well, and over the next two years they made some three dozen recordings with fiddle and guitar, ranging from the Old World ballad they called "I've Always Been a Rambler" to the Victorian pop song "Nobody's Darling" and the sober mortuary narratives of "The Red and Green Signal Lights" and "He Is Coming to Us Dead."

Grayson died when the car he was traveling in, or, rather, *on*—it was full, so he stood on its running board—collided with a log truck. His name has been kept alive by fellow musicians such as Wade Mainer, **Bill Monroe**, and **the Stanley Brothers** re-creating songs like "Train Forty-Five" and "Little Maggie."

G. B. Grayson (*left*) and a friend who shared his regard for old ballads, the singer, guitarist, and banjoist Clarence "Tom" Ashley.

EAST TEXAS SERENADERS

Instruments: fiddles, banjo, guitars, cello
Recording Debut: December 2, 1927

KEY RECORDINGS

Sweetest Flower (Waltz), **1927, 1937**
Combination Rag, **1927**
Acorn Stomp, **1928**
Three in One Two-Step, **1929**
East Texas Drag, **1937**
Arizona Stomp, **1937**

A profitable corner of the old-time record business was occupied by fiddlers and stringbands playing old-fashioned dance music: waltzes, one-steps, two-steps, and an occasional schottische. Whether such records were played at actual dances or were taken into the parlor instead for armchair listening is one of those apparently simple questions that historians haven't answered. But whatever use they were put to, they contain thousands of stirring performances from bands all over the South and Southwest.

Texas was especially fertile, supplying the Red Headed Fiddlers, Oscar & Doc Harper, Smith's Garage Fiddle Band, and many more. But the first band in the state to make a deep impression on wax was the East Texas Serenaders, from Smith and Wood Counties. They were essentially a typical small-town band that played for dances, ice-cream suppers, store openings, and other civic or community functions. What lifted them several notches above ordinary was the skill of their fiddler, Daniel Huggins Williams (1900–74). On their first record, he displayed his exquisite touch in the birdsong-like high passages of the waltz "Sweetest Flower," then on the other side, "Combination Rag," drove the band at a speed that might have deterred the doughtiest dancer.

Over the next three years, there were further records of that quality, like the irrepressibly toe-tapping "Acorn Stomp," but more pressing business than making music kept the band quiet for much of the '30s. They returned to a recording studio in 1937 with an augmented lineup that, particularly in pieces like "Say a Little Prayer for Me" or the bluesy "East Texas Drag," drew their ensemble sound closer to Western Swing. As well it might, for if we were to go looking for the seeds of Western Swing, we would certainly find some in the dance music of earlier Southwestern bands like the East Texas Serenaders.

The East Texas Serenaders, ca. 1928. *Standing*: John Munnerlyn (banjo), Huggins Williams (fiddle), Cloet Hamman (guitar). *Seated*: Jack Hopper (guitar), Henry Bogan (cello). The use of a bowed cello as a bass voice in the string ensemble was commonplace in the nineteenth century but began to fade in the recording era.

BASCOM LAMAR LUNSFORD

Dates: b. March 21, 1882, Mars Hill, NC; d. September 4, 1973, Asheville, NC
Instruments: banjo, fiddle, vocals
Recording Debut: March 15, 1924

KEY RECORDINGS

I Wish I Was a Mole in the Ground, **1924, 1928**
Mountain Dew, **1928**
Lulu Wall, **1928**
(Goodbye Dear Old) Stepstone, **1928**
Dry Bones, **1928**

It's a common belief that the musicians who made the earliest country records were mostly small-time farmers, coal miners, or cotton mill workers. In fact, their backgrounds were much more diverse. Many had white-collar jobs as doctors, ministers, teachers, realtors, county court clerks, and the like. Bascom Lamar Lunsford was first a high school teacher, then a lawyer, but posterity will remember him as a collector, promoter, and player of the old-time songs and banjo tunes of his native North Carolina. He himself recorded some of them in the 1920s, but in 1935 and 1949, at lengthy sessions at the Library of Congress, he reeled them off by the hundred. One of the most magical, rescued from rare-record obscurity when Harry Smith reissued it on his groundbreaking set *Anthology of American Folk Music* (1952), is "I Wish I Was a Mole in the Ground," blues-like in its random snapshots of a mountain life that was violent, beautiful, and, to a twenty-first-century eye, unutterably strange.

Lunsford may have been a less dramatic singer and musician than some of those around him, but his affable, conversational delivery made him a superb storyteller. He was also an early example of the public folklorist, broadcasting, performing for folklore societies, and talking up his region's musical culture in lectures and newspaper interviews. "We need the sad love songs of the past," he told the *Asheville Times* in 1926, before broadmindedly adding, "mixed in with the merry, racing jazz of today." He also founded the Mountain Dance and Folk Festival, which has drawn singers, pickers, and dancers to Asheville every year since 1928. Ancient film, possibly from the festival, shows him sawing away on fiddle, his second instrument. Among Lunsford's circle was Samantha Bumgarner of Sylva, North Carolina, whose 1924 fiddle and banjo tunes were the first old-time recordings by a woman.

Bascom Lamar Lunsford (*right*) with the singer and banjoist Obray Ramsey, one of the performers at the Asheville Mountain Dance and Folk Festival, c. 1960.

HOYT MING & HIS PEP STEPPERS

Instruments: fiddle, mandolin, guitar
Recording Debut: February 13, 1928

KEY RECORDINGS
Indian War Whoop, **1928**
Old Red, **1928**
White Mule, **1928**
Tupelo Blues, **1928**

In making records, old-time musicians were committing their songs and tunes to an unforeseeable future—sometimes to an afterlife they could scarcely have guessed at. When Hoyt Ming, from Choctaw County, Mississippi, fiddled his "Indian War Whoop" for Victor Records producer Ralph Peer (who mislabeled him "Floyd Ming"), he lit a tiny powder trail. It would snake through the decades, to catch fire in 2000 in the Coen brothers' film *O Brother, Where Art Thou?*, where John Hartford plays it as a torchlit posse delivers a gangster to jail. It came alight again, in its original recording, in 2023, in Martin Scorsese's *Killers of the Flower Moon*—which also recovers another Ming piece, "Tupelo Blues," played for a wedding by fiddler Rayna Gellert and friends.

Hoyt Ming (1902–85) was a quiet man who played music for a while at local dances with his guitar-playing wife, Rozelle (1906–83), until they were deterred by the drinking and violence and returned to their life as potato farmers. But the spell of "Indian War Whoop" would not quit. Long before the Coens and Scorsese, it was chosen by Harry Smith for his *Anthology of American Folk Music* (1952), wherein its jagged melody and stamping rhythm would entrance two or three generations of listeners. The Mings themselves had been in the movies too, playing (off-screen) in a fairground sequence in the 1976 film *Ode to Billy Joe*, inspired by Bobbie Gentry's enigmatic country song and shot where it was based, in Mississippi.

About that time, Hoyt and Rozelle represented their state at the National Folk Festival and made an album, *New Hot Times*. They enjoyed the attention but were bemused that it was all based on four tunes, an hour's work almost half a century in the past.

The Pep Steppers, 1927: Hoyt on fiddle, his wife, Rozelle, on guitar, his older brother Troy on mandolin, and, to call the dance figures, Andrew D. Coggin.

THE PICKARD FAMILY

Instruments: harmonica, Jew's harp, piano, guitars, vocals
Recording Debut: March 31, 1927

KEY RECORDINGS

Kitty Wells, **1927, 1930**
Walking in the Parlor [Obed Pickard Jew's harp solo], **1927**
Rabbit in the Pea Patch, **1928, 1929**
Buffalo Gals, **1929**
Behind the Parlor Door, **1929**
Good-Bye Mr. Greenback, **1930**

Obed "Dad" Pickard (1874–1954) was an expert player of the Jew's harp (mouthbow) who also sang and blew harmonica; "Mom" (Leila May Wilson Pickard, 1885–1972) played piano; two or three of their kids sang and picked guitar. They hailed from Tennessee but could have been from anywhere. Their material came as if from a national old-time songbook, and they performed it in no particular regional style or accent. Some songs were extended jokes ("She Never Came Back") or tall tales like the horror saga of "My Old Boarding House": "*Oh, the doughnuts they are wooden / And you have limberger puddin' / We kneel in prayer before we go to grub*" (a popular theme, given different readings by **Ernest V. Stoneman, Gid Tanner, Charlie Poole**, and many other old-time artists). Other pieces came from the minstrel era, when white composers' fantasies of African American life produced the tearstained elegy "Kitty Wells" and the comic violence of "Get Away from That Window" (the Pickards' retitling of "Razors in De Air"). But the Family ventured no farther down that road, and they stopped short of the blues. Just once, they spoke to the present rather than the past, in the Depression song "Good-Bye Mr. Greenback."

You might say they were a straiter-laced **Carter Family**. Most histories of country music say little about them at all, but the Pickards' affable friendly-neighbor approach to what Dad called "old time Hick and Hoe down Hill Billy Songs" won large radio audiences, first on the *Grand Ole Opry*, then on stations in Chicago, Philadelphia, and New York, in prestigious shows like the *Lucky Strike Hour* and the *National Farm & Home Hour*. In the '30s, they were heard (like the Carters) from the Mexican border station XERA, and later they moved to California.

"Perhaps if it weren't for radio," wrote Dad Pickard, introducing this 1929 songbook, "we would never have been heard outside the confines of [our] little country town in the Tennessee Hills." The Family's popularity on air was replicated on disc: between 1927 and 1930, they made more than thirty recordings, some of them, such as "She'll Be Comin' 'Round the Mountain" or "The Little Red Caboose Behind the Train," issued on ten or more labels.

CLARENCE ASHLEY

Dates: Thomas Clarence Ashley (Clarence Earl McCurry), b. September 29, 1895, Bristol, TN; d. June 2, 1967, Winston-Salem, NC
Instruments: banjo, guitar, vocals
Recording Debut: February 2, 1928

KEY RECORDINGS

The Coo-Coo Bird, **1929**
Three Men Went a Hunting [with Byrd Moore's Hot Shots], **1929**
The House Carpenter, **1930**
My Sweet Farm Girl, **1931**
Greenback Dollar [with Gwyn Foster], **1933**

Clarence Ashley had a long and varied career, and he crammed into its first stage an extraordinary amount of music making. He sang and played guitar, with banjoist Dock Walsh and harmonica player Garley Foster, in a popular stringband, the Carolina Tar Heels. With his own banjo, playing modally in what he called "sawmill tuning," he gave compelling renditions of mountain folk songs and Old World ballads like "The House Carpenter." With guitarist Byrd Moore's Hot Shots, he sang "Three Men Went a Hunting," which really is an old-time song since it can be traced back to Shakespearian England. In a group with Foster, fiddler Clarence Greene, and a few other friends, the Blue Ridge Mountain Entertainers, he recorded everything from dance tunes to blues to comedy sketches. All of this within three years. Two years later, he and Foster reunited to make a series of fine blues sides such as "Sideline Blues," "Bay Rum Blues," and "Times Ain't Like They Used to Be."

By 1933, of course, times *weren't* like they used to be, and those recordings were his last for a quarter of a century. But he had the musical and comedic skills of a seasoned entertainer, and as late as the '50s, while working with **the Stanley Brothers**, he was delivering blackface routines that he had learned forty years earlier as a young man in a traveling medicine show in eastern Tennessee. In the early '60s, music historians visited him to record two Folkways albums of *Old-Time Music at Clarence Ashley's* and happened to encounter a young guitar-playing associate named Doc Watson. This led to appearances at the Newport Folk Festival and other focal points of the folk revival, where Ashley's versatility and zestful anecdotes earned him the affection of younger players, and his songs took on new lives.

Clarence "Tom" Ashley (guitar) with his fellow Carolina Tar Heels, "Dock" Walsh (banjo) and Garley Foster (harmonica and guitar). "Over at Tom's House," a humorous sketch from 1931, was issued on Sears, Roebuck's Conqueror label.

BOB MILLER

Dates: b. September 20, 1895, Ansonia, CT; d. August 26, 1955, New York, NY
Instruments: piano, vocals
Recording Debut: August 17, 1928

KEY RECORDINGS

Eleven Cent Cotton Forty Cent Meat, **1928–29**
Little Red Caboose Behind the Train, **1929–32**
Twenty-One Years, **1929–32**
Rockin' Alone (in an Old Rockin' Chair), **1932–33**
Seven Years with the Wrong Woman, **1932**

Bob Miller cuts an unusual figure on the country music stage. He played piano (uncommon), he was Jewish (rare), and politically he appears to have leaned to the left (also rare). Nevertheless, he wrote many of the bestselling country songs of the '30s and '40s, encouraged new acts by supplying them with material and producing their records, and had a decade-long career making records himself.

The first of these was "Eleven Cent Cotton Forty Cent Meat" ("*How in the world can a poor man eat?*"), a caustic litany of agricultural hardship. It was credited to "Bob Ferguson," perhaps because Miller was already known in rather different quarters as a Memphis-based writer and publisher of jazz tunes and sometime bandleader on the Mississippi riverboat *Idlewild*. Or possibly because he had filched the title and several of the verses from a poem, ostensibly written by either a Texan housewife or a Shreveport high school girl, that had appeared in many newspapers during 1926–27. Thereafter, his topical compositions seem to have been his own, and there were many of them: "The Farmer's Letter to the President," "Dry Voters and Wet Drinkers," "Farm Relief Blues," "The Ohio Prison Fire," "Bank Failures," "The Death of Jack 'Legs' Diamond" . . . and these are just a small section of his song folio, among evocations of nature like "When the White Azaleas Start Blooming," comic novelties about mules, and prison laments such as "Ninety-Nine Years" ("*is almost for life*") that were widely recorded by other artists. He often claimed to have written thousands of songs, but the real figure is probably closer to several hundred, a portfolio that in later years he managed from his office at 1619 Broadway—the famous Brill Building, where so many beloved pop songs were written in the '60s.

Bob Miller as an up-and-coming young songwriter and bandleader, 1923. “My buddy Homer Gentry” was a flautist and fellow orchestra leader in Memphis.

HOBART SMITH

Dates: b. May 10, 1897, near Saltville, VA; d. January 11, 1965, Saltville, VA
Instruments: banjo, guitar, fiddle, piano, vocals
Recording Debut: August 29, 1942

KEY RECORDINGS

The Cuckoo (Bird), **1942**, **1963**
Claude Allen, **1959**
Railroad Bill, **1959**
Graveyard Blues, **1959**
The Devil's Dream, **1960**

Not all the great old-time musicians recorded in the 1920s or '30s. Some didn't care to, some lived beyond the reach of talent scouts, and some were simply too busy making a living. Hobart Smith started out as a farmer, then became a wagon driver, house painter, and butcher for a canned-meat company. Apart from trips away, mostly in later years, he spent his entire life in Saltville, Virginia (within easy reach, in 1927, of the Bristol recording session, had he known or cared about it). Music was important to him, but it didn't dominate his existence. His main instrument was the banjo, but for many years he didn't own one. He started when he was seven, learning mostly from an itinerant, John Greer—"the best man I ever heard, and I patterned after him." Later, he took up guitar, instructed by older players, some African American, and fiddle, his chief tutor an ex-slave named Jim Spencer. He also played a little piano.

By the age of twenty, Smith had progressed from local music making to playing (and dancing) on traveling minstrel shows, where he met **Clarence Ashley**. After he and his sister, Texas Gladden, a highly regarded singer, appeared at the folk festival in White Top, Virginia, they were invited to perform at the White House. In 1942, Alan Lomax recorded him for the Library of Congress, and over the next couple of decades, the folklorist made more recordings, booked him for concerts, and recommended him to record labels. In the '50s, Smith had six tunes on the influential LP *Instrumental Music of the Southern Appalachians*, and later there was an album for Folk-Legacy. He was an idiosyncratically superb banjo player, a guitarist with an acute feeling for the blues, a lively dance fiddler, and a moving ballad singer.

Hobart Smith traveled to New York in 1946 to record some of his songs and tunes for Disc. The Folk-Legacy LP shown here dates from 1964.

I WANT TO BE
A COWBOY'S SWEET
by
PATSY MONTANA
DOLLY
MILLIE

THE RADIO YEARS
THE 1930s TO WORLD WAR II

In the 1920s, buyers of "Old Time Songs" or "Old Familiar Tunes" had constituted the first market for recorded country music. By the early '30s, however, the Depression had seriously damaged the disc business. Most people were mired in the deep swamp of hard times and were spending their meager cash on food, rent, gas, and other things that were more urgently necessary than records. They had one recourse: radio. There, the entertainment was free. There, too, the musicians who had once populated the record catalogs could find a stage, and the advertising sponsors, to reach an audience and maybe make a living.

BRADLEY KINCAID

Dates: William Bradley Kincaid, b. July 13, 1895, Garrard County, KY; d. September 23, 1989, Springfield, OH
Instruments: guitar, vocals
Recording Debut: December 19, 1927

KEY RECORDINGS

The Fatal Wedding, **1927–31**
Sweet Kitty Wells, **1927**
Barbara Allen, **1928–30**
The Blind Girl, **1929–34**
The Red River Valley, **1929–34**

Present-day admirers of old-time country music tend to be attracted by the excitement of tearaway stringbands or the edgy humor of hillbilly blues. Its original audience had broader tastes, and no artist demonstrates this more clearly than Bradley Kincaid. His chosen field was the old songs and ballads remembered by folk in his native Kentucky. He collected them with the diligence of a folklorist, but with a different purpose—not to imprison them in a book, but to circulate them, through radio, to a double audience: people who remembered them and enjoyed hearing them again, and others who had never encountered them but were captivated by their evocation of an older, disappearing America.

For both groups, songs like "The Fatal Wedding," "The Blind Girl," "Barbara Allen," or "The Little Rosewood Casket"—some drawn from published compositions of the late nineteenth century, others with longer, half-lost pedigrees—held stories of romance and regret passed down from a less complicated time than the hectic 1920s. Kincaid told them plainly, simply accompanied on his "Hound Dog guitar," to a national radio listenership—first on the WLS *National Barn Dance*, subsequently on other stations—then on records, then again in little songbooks called *My Favorite Mountain Ballads*, which he sold by mail order. He embodied his role of old-time songster so completely that he was able, decades later, to emerge from retirement and record his songs again on LPs for a new and no-less-appreciative audience. In 1971, he was inducted into the Nashville Songwriters Hall of Fame: an odd tribute, since most of the songs for which he was known were much older than he was. He was less a composer than an editor and arranger, but such men played a vital role in the early media history of country music.

Bradley Kincaid was billed as "one of the first of the mountain ballad singers to be heard over the air."

CARSON ROBISON

Dates: b. August 4, 1890, Chetopa, KS;
d. March 24, 1957, Poughkeepsie, NY
Instruments: guitar, harmonica, whistling, vocals
Recording Debut: May 1924 [with Wendell Hall]

KEY RECORDINGS

My Blue Ridge Mountain Home [with Vernon Dalhart], **1927–28**

Barnacle Bill, the Sailor, **1928** *

Goin' Back to Texas, **1929–32** *

When It's Springtime in the Rockies, **1929–32** *

Sleepy Rio Grande, **1929–32** *

* with Frank Luther

It was ironic that his last hit, "Life Gits Tee-jus, Don't It?" (1948), was about a fella sittin' around doin' nothin'. Few men in country music kept busier or more creative than Carson Robison. Arriving in New York in 1924 as a singer, guitarist, and whistler experienced in Midwestern theater and radio, he was commissioned by Victor to work with their new dispenser of old-time Southern songs, **Vernon Dalhart**. Robison played guitar and sang tenor harmony with him on hundreds of records, writing many of the "event songs" that Dalhart's buyers enjoyed, such as "The John T. Scopes Trial" (creationism vs. evolution), "The Wreck of the 1256" (fate vs. train), and "The Wreck of the Shenandoah" (fate vs. airship). After that uneasy four-year partnership ended, Robison collaborated with the multitalented singer (and skilled Dalhart imitator) Frank Luther (1900–80) on hundreds more recordings.

In 1932, Robison formed his Pioneers, with banjoists/guitarists John and Bill Mitchell and singer Pearl Pickens Mitchell. Widely heard on US radio, this unit also toured the UK three times in the '30s, making scores of records, transcription discs for Radio Luxembourg, and entertaining short films for Pathé. No other hillbilly artist made such an impact on British audiences, who largely derived their notions of the genre from Robison's astute mixture of cowboy songs, comedy numbers, and evocations of the American landscape.

In the later '30s, Robison's Western playlets and their campfire singalong settings could not compete with the tougher short stories of honky-tonk, but he had a World War II bestseller with his response to the Japanese attack on Pearl Harbor, "1942 Turkey in the Straw." "Rockin' and Rollin' with Grandmaw" (1956) proved he remained aware of country music's shifting tectonic plates.

"Francis Crowell and Luther Woods" was one of the many pseudonyms used on records by Frank Luther and Carson Robison. Working for so many labels, the duo's identity had to be masked to deceive rival companies and potential customers alike.

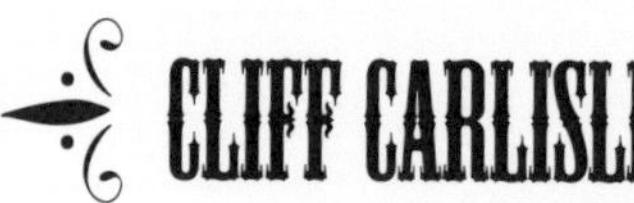

CLIFF CARLISLE

Dates: Clifford Raymond Carlisle, b. May 6, 1904, Taylorsville, KY; d. April 2, 1983, Lexington, KY
Instruments: guitar, vocals
Recording Debut: February 25, 1930

KEY RECORDINGS

Just a Lonely Hobo, **1930–31**
When the Cactus Is in Bloom, **1931**
Shanghai Rooster Yodel, **1931**
That Nasty Swing, **1936**
A Wild Cat Woman and a Tom Cat Man, **1936**
Cowboy's Dying Dream, **1937**

"My music is a cross between hillbilly and blues," Cliff Carlisle would say in later years, adding, because he also played in a Hawaiian style, "even Hawaiian music has a sort of blues to it." No one did more to popularize the bluesy hillbilly/Hawaiian sound of the Dobro™ acoustic steel resonator guitar, a predecessor of the electric pedal steel guitar. Playing it with a steel slide, as Hawaiian and some African American musicians did, Carlisle lent a propulsive zing to fast numbers and a dreamy moonlight mood to slow ones.

A contemporary of **Jimmie Rodgers**, and at least as versatile a singer, Carlisle echoed the other man's yodeling but ventured further down the red-lit streets of erotic song, creating witty metaphors for sex out of wild cats and crowing roosters. In "Mouse's Ear Blues" (1933), a duet with his guitar-playing younger brother Bill, their hesitant laughter suggests they can't quite believe they're getting away with this extended metaphor for defloration.

From the late 1920s to the end of the '30s, Cliff was a familiar voice on radio, first on the Louisville stations WHAS and WLAP—paired for a while with guitarist Wilbur Ball as the Lullaby Larkers—and then with Bill on WBT in Charlotte, North Carolina. He also made hundreds of records, ranging from blues and hobo songs to comic novelties such as **Bob Miller**'s "Seven Years with the Wrong Woman" (1932) and the old ballad "Black Jack David" (1939), later taken up by Bob Dylan. After World War II, Cliff worked with Bill in the family group the Carlisles, who were popular on the *Grand Ole Opry* and had hits with "Too Old to Cut the Mustard" and "No Help Wanted," but in the mid-'50s, in uncertain health, he retired to the peace of fishing and painting.

Cowboy boots and six-gun were parts of the Western image adopted by many country artists in the '30s and later. Cliff Carlisle inscribed this photo to record collector Eugene W. Earle, who was the first to document Cliff's life and recording career.

THE GIRLS OF THE GOLDEN WEST

Dates: Mildred Fern Good, b. April 11, 1913, Mt. Carmel, IL; d. May 2, 1993; Dorothy Laverne Good, b. December 11, 1915, Mt. Carmel, IL; d. November 12, 1967
Instruments: guitar, vocals
Recording Debut: July 28, 1933

KEY RECORDINGS

Started Out from Texas, **1933**
Old Chisholm Trail, **1934**
Bucking Broncho, **1934**
Roll Along, Prairie Moon, **1935**
I Want to Be a Real Cowboy Girl, **1935, 1938**

"The Girls of the Golden West" was the professional billing of Millie and Dolly Good (originally Goad). It was not an obvious choice: they hailed from southern Illinois and grew up in St. Louis, where they began their radio career as teenagers on KMOX. So a creative copywriter gave them an appropriate backstory, beginning in the fictional town of Muleshoe, Texas. Their Western provenance established, Millie and Dolly needed no style consultant to tell them how to dress; cowboys and cowgirls wore buckskin, boots, neckerchiefs, fringes—everyone knew that. Garbed for ranch and bunkhouse, the Goods effortlessly took on the role of country music's first Western sister act, decorous pinups from the prairie, sweetly harmonizing on songs of the range.

"Golden West" is an idealization, and their songs generally were too, telling their stories in the language of the cowboy novel and the Western B movie. A rare exception is "Bucking Broncho," a cowboy romance whose double entendres have no parallel in their work. They originated few of their numbers; mostly they bought songs from other artists or adapted them from records, like "That Silver Haired Daddy of Mine" from **Gene Autry**. Their repertoire was loaded with keywords like "Texas," "cowgirl," "cowboy," "prairie," and "trail," but now and then they relaxed the Western emphasis to sing a popular piece like "Red Sails in the Sunset." What mattered was that the song worked as a harmony number, with their trademark harmonized yodeling. On "Roll Along, Prairie Moon," one of them sings a wordless high part that sounds for all the world like a Hawaiian guitar (anticipating **the DeZurik Sisters**).

Milly and Dolly soon retired into family life, but twenty-some years later they remade their old songs, and more, for a series of Bluebonnet LPs. Time's touch upon them had been featherlight.

Sweethearts of the Rodeo: Millie and (*right*) Dolly Good. They made all their own costumes. Sometimes they toted six-guns (but with no bullets in them).

RED FOLEY

Dates: Clyde Julian Foley, b. June 17, 1910, Blue Lick, KY; d. September 19, 1968, Fort Wayne, IN
Instruments: guitar, vocals
Recording Debut: April 11, 1933

KEY RECORDINGS

Old Shep, **1935, 1941**
Tennessee Saturday Night, **1948**
Chattanooga Shoe Shine Boy, **1950**
Sugar-Foot Rag [with Hank Garland], **1950**
Peace in the Valley, **1951**

Personable and versatile, Red Foley made his name through radio, first on the WLS *National Barn Dance* in the early '30s. He was the featured singer in a group from around Berea, Kentucky, the Cumberland Ridge Runners, organized by the local folklorist John Lair to convey the flavor of Appalachian music to the program's Midwestern audience. Over the next quarter century or so, Foley had spells, often of several years, on other radio, and later TV, programs: the *Renfro Valley Barn Dance*, WLS again, the *Grand Ole Opry*, and the Springfield, Missouri, *Ozark Jubilee*.

Apart from "Old Shep," a tearjerker about the life and (spoiler alert) death of a boy's beloved dog, later taken up by Elvis Presley, Foley's early recordings may strike today's listeners as rather colorless, but those he made in the late '40s and '50s—mainly in Nashville, where he was one of the first country singers to record, in January 1945—are another matter altogether. An admirer of Black music, he chose a number of songs in the boogie-woogie style of the period. (He even made a track, not issued at the time, with the African American singer-pianist Cecil Gant, a Nashvillean and fellow Decca artist.) Following a different wind across the landscape of popular music, he recorded country songs with the Andrews Sisters; pursuing another, he accrued rockabilly credibility with the aid of the brilliant Nashville session guitarists Hank Garland, who cowrote their hit "Sugar-Foot Rag," and Hardrock Gunter, composer of "Birmingham Bounce," a long-stay no. 1 on the country chart. These progressive excursions were balanced by more conventional duets with **Kitty Wells** and **Ernest Tubb** and by his fondness for gospel music, displayed in "Peace in the Valley," a million-seller and another song liked by Elvis, and in the 1956 album *Beyond the Sunset*.

The Cumberland Ridge Runners, ca. 1933: Homer "Slim" Miller (fiddle), John Lair (harmonica), Karl Davis (mandolin), singer Linda Parker, Red Foley (bass), Harty Taylor (guitar). Karl and Harty were a popular duo in their own right. *Stand By!* was WLS's weekly magazine.

LULU BELLE & SCOTTY

Dates: Myrtle Eleanor Cooper, December 24, 1913, Boone, NC; d. February 8, 1999, Spruce Pine, NC; Scott Wiseman, b. November 8, 1909, Ingalls, NC; d. January 31, 1981, Ingalls, NC
Instruments: guitar, vocals (Lulu Belle); banjo, guitar, harmonica, vocals (Scotty)
Recording Debut: March 1934

KEY RECORDINGS

Wish I Was a Single Girl Again, **1939**
Mountain Dew, **1939**
Remember Me, **1940**
Have I Told You Lately That I Love You, **1944**
I'm No Communist, **1951**

In the '30s, Lulu Belle and Scotty were a popular act on the *National Barn Dance*. Like many of the Chicago program's cast, they were from somewhere else: North Carolina, where Scotty had found old songs—like "Get Along Home Cindy," "Wish I Was a Single Girl Again," and the moonshine ditty "Mountain Dew"—that conveyed a flavor of rustic Appalachia to the far-flung WLS audience. In time he would write his own material: heart songs like "Have I Told You Lately That I Love You" or "Remember Me" ("*when candle-lights are gleaming . . . remember me at the close of a long, long day*").

When Lulu Belle first joined the show, she sang with **Red Foley**, but she and Scotty quickly became a couple, not only professionally but personally. For a while, this was hidden from the listeners—until Lulu Belle was pregnant with their first baby. "We started singing a little song called 'Somebody's Coming to Our House,'" she said, "and the next day the presents started arriving." Thanks to their attractive image and radio fame, they appeared in several of the hillbilly movies that were a fad in the late '30s and early '40s, and they continued to make records, such as the buoyant free-enterprise number "I'm No Communist": "*I like this private ownership, I want to be left alone—Let the government run its business, and let me run my own.*" Somewhat improbably, their 1949 recording "Spearmint on the Bedpost" may have been the source of the British skiffle artist Lonnie Donegan's 1955 hit "Does Your Chewing Gum Lose Its Flavour (on the Bedpost Overnight?)." They retired in 1958 but satisfied their fans with albums and personal appearances for another twenty years, with Lulu Belle meanwhile serving two terms in the North Carolina state legislature.

As one of WLS's most popular acts, Lulu Belle and Scotty earned the rare privilege of a full-color cover on their songbook. For many radio artists, songbook sales were a major part of their income.

PATSY MONTANA

Dates: Rubye Rose Blevins, b. October 30, 1908, Beaudry, AR; d. May 3, 1996, San Jacinto, CA
Instruments: fiddle, vocals
Recording Debut: November 4, 1932

KEY RECORDINGS

Montana Plains, **1933**
I Wanna Be a Cowboy's Sweetheart, **1935**, **1941**
Woman's Answer to Nobody's Darling, **1936**
I Wanna Be a Western Cowgirl, **1939**
Swing Time Cowgirl, **1940**

Patsy Montana was the first woman in country music to have a really big hit. "I Wanna Be a Cowboy's Sweetheart" is sometimes said to have sold a million copies, but it didn't; with one exception (by **Vernon Dalhart**), no country record before World War II is documented as reaching that figure. But its sales were considerable, establishing Patsy as a major country music personality.

How she got into the business reads like the plot of a Hollywood musical. "I had heard **the Girls of the Golden West** over WLS and wrote them my first fan letter. I admired their Western singing and harmony. Their manager asked me to come by and see him." She did, and she was asked to audition for the Prairie Ramblers, a four-piece Kentucky stringband that was doing well on WLS but needed a girl singer. She never went home.

The Prairie Ramblers, like all the leading WLS acts, were indefatigable record makers, and between 1933 and 1940 they made scores of discs featuring Patsy's winsome singing and yodeling. They were evocative, upbeat songs about life in the saddle, their titles bristling with keywords like "hills," "plains," "cowboy," and, unsurprisingly, "Montana." The Ramblers and Patsy covered thousands of miles touring with the *National Barn Dance* troupe, meeting folks who knew them from shows like *Smile-a-While*, which greeted WLS listeners at 5:30 every morning.

In the '40s, no longer with the Ramblers, she found it difficult to be old-style in a fast-changing musical landscape and retired into family life. By the '70s, however, she was venerated as a founding figure, and she sang on the *Opry*, made albums, appeared at folk festivals, and toured overseas. Wherever people honored Western music, Patsy would be there, and she is enshrined in the National Cowgirl Hall of Fame.

Patsy Montana and the Prairie Ramblers, ca. 1935. *Standing*: Jack Taylor (bass), Tex Atchison (fiddle). *Seated*: Salty Holmes (harmonica, guitar), Chick Hurt (mandola). On records, the Ramblers (without Patsy) were sometimes billed instead as the Sweet Violet Boys, to deliver material a little edgier than they could get away with on radio, such as "You Oughta See My Fannie Dance."

THE DELMORE BROTHERS

Dates: Alton Delmore, b. December 25, 1908, Elkmont, AL; d. June 9, 1964, Huntsville, AL
Rabon Delmore, b. December 3, 1916, Elkmont, AL; d. December 4, 1952, Athens, AL
Instruments: guitar, tenor guitar, vocals
Recording Debut: October 28, 1931

KEY RECORDINGS

Brown's Ferry Blues, **1933**
Gonna Lay Down My Old Guitar, **1933**
I've Got the Big River Blues, **1933**
Freight Train Boogie, **1946**
Blues Stay Away from Me, **1949**

The new style of "country crooning" that arose in the '30s was led by two brothers from northern Alabama, Alton and Rabon Delmore. As with so many "brother acts," their voices had a natural blend, and they developed a warm, soft-edged, fur-lined harmony. Amid the boisterous stringbands and high, lonesome banjo songsters of the late 1920s and early '30s, they stood out as offering a fresh way with country songs: intimate, in your ear rather than in your face. After an obscure debut in 1931, they began making records seriously in 1933, their early success with the smutty, catchy "Brown's Ferry Blues" ensuring them a career on Bluebird discs throughout the decade and beyond. They sang blues, love songs, and stories of tragedy, but it was the sound as much as the content that captured listeners, the perfectly attuned voices gracefully underpinned by two mellow guitars, Rabon picking the tenor, Alton the standard.

While on the *Grand Ole Opry*, they and the show's outstanding personality, **Uncle Dave Macon**, formed a surprising but successful combination. They traveled together, and the brothers accompanied the old man on records. But Rabon's drinking made him erratic, and when the duo lost their *Opry* slot, they found it hard to obtain another until the mid-'40s, when they landed one in Cincinnati on the WLW *Boone County Jamboree*. Their records for the local indie King—in settings with Wayne Raney's harmonica and, increasingly, electric guitars—were even more successful than their previous ones—something few veterans of the early years would achieve. The brothers also sang in a popular and influential gospel quartet, the Brown's Ferry Four. Their career was terminated by Rabon's death; Alton retired to write and composed a revealing account of their years together, published posthumously as *Truth Is Stranger Than Publicity*.

Rabon (*left*) and Alton Delmore. This was their stock picture for years in the catalog of Bluebird Records, for whom they made almost sixty discs between 1933 and 1940.

LONNIE GLOSSON

Dates: Lonnie Elonzo Glosson, b. February 14, 1908, Judsonia, AR; d. March 2, 2001, Searcy, AR
Instruments: harmonica, guitar, vocals
Recording Debut: December 1931

KEY RECORDINGS

The Fox Chase, 1931, **1936**
Arkansas Hard Luck Blues, **1936**
West Bound Rocket, **1947**
I Want My Mama, **1958**

Generations of folk, blues, and country musicians have made the harmonica their first and often their favorite instrument. It owes much of this popularity to Lonnie Glosson. He and his sidekick Wayne Raney sold harmonicas and instruction books to hundreds of thousands of mail-order customers, on radio programs syndicated all over the United States and Canada. Years later, they reenacted their spiel for an English TV documentary: "Neighbors, we're going to be demonstrating the talking harmonica and telling you how you too can have one just exactly like the ones your old friends Lonnie Glosson and Wayne Raney play. For this entire deal, the talking harmonica and the play-by-ear instructions, just send your name and address and three dollars and ninety-eight cents to BBC Television network, London, England."

Glosson, who had learned to play harmonica from his mother, Cora, first performed on WMOX in St Louis, moving in 1930 to the WLS *National Barn Dance*. His first record coupled the two sound pictures all rural harmonica players can paint: a foxhunt and a train. Later he came up with "I Want My Mama," simulating a plaintive child. He and Raney—a fellow Arkansawyer, thirteen years younger—teamed up in the '40s, when their twin harmonicas were often heard, uncredited, on King records by **the Delmore Brothers**, such as "Blues Stay Away from Me," and on their own hits like their composition "Why Don't You Haul Off and Love Me," sung by Raney. For a while, they concentrated on radio and merchandising, based in Cincinnati and sponsored by Wm. Kratt harmonicas, but then Glosson returned to the road, often working in schools, where he performed country and gospel numbers with his guitar alongside the harmonica favorites. He and Raney reunited in the '80s to re-create old-time rural radio for a new generation.

Lonnie Glosson in later life, when he could still be found on the road every year. As well as their harmonica salesmanship, Glosson and Raney advertised a "Picture Way To Play Guitar in 10 Days or Your Money Back."

THE WESTERNERS

Instruments: fiddle, accordion, piano, guitar, bass, vocals
Recording Debut: October 13, 1933

KEY RECORDINGS

Ridin' Down That Old Texas Trail, **1934**
Brown Skin Gal, **1934**
Rancho Grande, **1934**
South of the Border, **1939**
Rock and Rye Polka, **1940**
My Adobe Hacienda, **1941**

You won't read much about the Westerners in country music histories, but in the '30s and '40s they were one of the hottest acts in rural radio. Like their contemporaries the Prairie Ramblers, they appealed both as a versatile stringband and as the backing group for a vivacious female singer. Their match for **Patsy Montana** was Louise Massey (1902–83), and her gang included brothers Dott (a.k.a. Curt, 1910–91) on fiddle and Allen (1907–83) on guitar; her husband, Milt Mabie (1900–73), on string bass; and accordionist/pianist Larry Wellington (1903–73). On a few records, the band accompanied their father, Henry "Dad" Massey (1866–1949), a sprightly old-time fiddler. Curt's fiddling was in a newer swing idiom, and he doubled on hot trumpet.

The Masseys were born in Midland, Texas, but grew up as a farm family in Roswell, New Mexico. Their first billet as a band was in 1928 on KMBC in Kansas City. Five years later, they moved to the WLS *National Barn Dance*, and from there to prestige radio spots in New York. In 1939, they returned to WLS, having developed the skill of offering something for everyone; their repertoire embraced Western songs, polkas, songs in Spanish, hoedown numbers, and jazzed-up kids' songs like "Mary Had a Little Lamb" or "Polly Wolly Doodle." The lineup was expanded on recording sessions with electric and steel guitars, drums, and reeds. They sounded immensely polished, if at times a tad bland, but some of their recordings were zippy Western Swing, if less jazzy than **Bob Wills** or **Milton Brown**.

In the later '40s, Louise and Milt retired to a life on the ranch. Curt and Allen worked in California, where Curt became musical director for the hugely popular network TV programs *The Beverly Hillbillies* and *Petticoat Junction*.

The Westerners inscribed this photograph to WLS program director George C. Biggar. Elaborate Western dress was invisible to a radio audience, but WLS sent its artists out on tour and to county fairs, where they would be seen by tens of thousands.

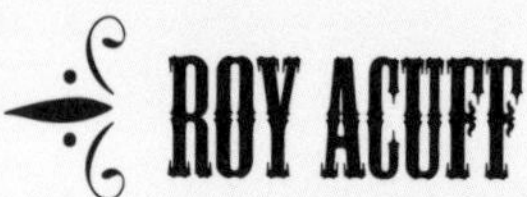

ROY ACUFF

Dates: Roy Claxton Acuff, b. September 15, 1903, Maynardville, TN: d. November 23, 1992, Nashville, TN
Instruments: fiddle, vocals
Recording Debut: October 20, 1936

KEY RECORDINGS

Great Speckle(d) Bird, **1936**
Wabash Cannonball, **1936**
Freight Train Blues, **1936**
Old Age Pension Check, **1939**
Wreck on the Highway, **1942**
Fireball Mail, **1942**
Pins and Needles, **1942**

In later life, Roy Acuff was regarded as the Grand Old Man of the *Grand Ole Opry*, of which he was a cast member for half a century. He was also, as joint proprietor of Acuff–Rose, Inc., a godfather of the Nashville music-publishing business. But although he played down his own talent—"I'm a seller, not a singer"—he owned one of the most influential voices in country music.

It was first heard in its sober fervor in 1936, at a session that produced the immortal country songs "Wabash Cannonball" and "Freight Train Blues," and a sacred number that his followers would never thereafter let him forget to sing, the parable (from Jeremiah 12:9) of the "Great Speckled Bird." Previously known chiefly to the radio audience of the *Mid-Day Merry-Go-Round* on WNOX in Knoxville, Acuff now became famous throughout the country, hitching his wagon to the *Opry*'s star in 1938, making movies in the '40s, and gathering about him in his Smoky Mountain Boys long-serving sidemen like fiddler Howdy Forrester and banjo and Dobro™ player "Bashful Brother Oswald" (Pete Kirby). He twice ran for election, both times unsuccessfully, as the governor of Tennessee.

Like many of his peers, he was edged aside in the '50s by rock 'n' roll; perhaps it was a gesture of reconciliation that he participated with rock musicians, in 1972, in the Nitty Gritty Dirt Band's triple album *Will the Circle Be Unbroken?* He could afford to be generous, since ten years earlier he had been the first living musician to enter the Country Music Hall of Fame, and he held an unassailable position as a spokesman for Music City. In a celebrated incident, on the stage of the new *Opry* in 1974, he tutored the then president, Richard Nixon, in how to play the yo-yo.

The songs in this folio date it to around 1944—the year of Acuff's first sortie into politics, when he ran for office on the Republican ticket.

CLAYTON McMICHEN

Dates: b. January 26, 1900, Altoona, GA; d. January 4, 1970, Battletown, KY
Instruments: fiddle, vocals
Recording Debut: July 7, 1925

KEY RECORDINGS

Peach Picking Time Down in Georgia [with Jimmie Rodgers], **1932**
Farewell Blues, **1937**
Bile Dem Cabbage Down, **1937**
Georgiana Moon, **1937**
I'm Gonna Learn to Swing, **1938**

When the record business tanked in the early '30s, McMichen parlayed the fame he'd accrued with **the Skillet-Lickers** into radio jobs on WCKY in Covington, Kentucky; WLW in Cincinnati; WHAS in Louisville; and other stations in the region. For a while, he continued to work with **Riley Puckett**, but his ambition was to staff his Georgia Wildcats with younger, more sophisticated musicians, such as guitarist Hoyt "Slim" Bryant (1908–2010). In 1932, he and Bryant accompanied **Jimmie Rodgers** on "Whippin' That Old TB" and McMichen's composition "Peach Picking Time Down in Georgia." Around this time, "Mac" was approached to go to Hollywood with **Gene Autry**, an offer he always regretted turning down.

For several years, Mac slogged around the Midwest, holding on to his title of National Fiddling Champion, focused on his dream of "makin' something out of hillbilly music, makin' it popular." In 1937, now under contract to Decca, he created a sleek arrangement of the jazz standard "Farewell Blues" that he came to regard as "the best record I ever made." "St. Louis Woman (Got Her Diamond in the Hock Shop Now)," an update of "St Louis Blues," and "I'm Gonna Learn to Swing" plainly stated Mac's disaffection for the old-time music he had once played, but he was savvy enough to accede to Decca's request for an album of old fiddle tunes.

Mac finally retired, for health reasons, in 1955. He was frequently interviewed by record collectors who didn't care about Mac the swinger, still less about his later years playing Dixieland jazz, but just wanted to talk about the Skillet-Lickers. He made one of his last public appearances at the 1964 Newport Folk Festival, where he was revered once again for a stage of his musical career that he thought little of and wanted to forget.

"Mac," the uptown swingster (*second from left*), with his brother-in-law Bert Layne (fiddle) and guitarists Jack Dunigan and (*standing*) Hoyt "Slim" Bryant, ca. 1931–32. The Gibson guitar company enthusiastically boosted country artists who used—and thus promoted—its products.

MAINER'S MOUNTAINEERS

Instruments: fiddle, banjo, guitars, vocals
Recording Debut: August 6, 1935

KEY RECORDINGS

Maple on the Hill, **1935**
Take Me in the Lifeboat, **1935**
Lights in the Valley, **1935**
Green Back Dollar [Daddy John Love solo], **1935**
New Lost Train Blues, **1936**
Country Blues, **1939**

Southern radio audiences in the '30s liked their hillbilly acts wide ranging and quick changing, their quarter-hour or half-hour programs packed with comedy numbers, blues, heart songs, hoedown tunes, and hymns. No band filled this bill more expertly than Mainer's Mountaineers. In 1934, they joined the cast of the *Crazy Barn Dance* on WBT in Charlotte, North Carolina, sponsored by the laxative company Crazy Water Crystals; the following year, they burst into the Bluebird Records catalog. Leader Joseph E. Mainer (1898–1971) played fiddle, his brother Wade (1907–2011) banjo, and Zeke Morris (1916–99) and Daddy John Love (1905–57) guitars. Wade and Zeke sang duets like their first release and biggest hit, "Maple on the Hill," and John delivered blue yodels in the manner of **Jimmie Rodgers** over a driving flat-picked guitar. Over four years and sixty recordings, different lineups of Mountaineers, involving fifteen musicians, deftly mixed new songs and galvanic revisions of ones recorded in the previous decade by **the Skillet-Lickers**, **the Georgia Yellow Hammers**, or **Charlie Poole**, such as "Watermelon on the Vine," "The Old and Faded Picture," or "Take Me Home to the Sweet Sunny South." Wade and Zeke pursued a separate and even more prolific recording career with their duets.

On various North Carolina stations, the Mainers were listeners' favorites well into the '40s, while in public appearances J. E. was faithful to the entertainment forms of his youth like comic playlets and blackface routines. By the '50s, that seemed rather old hat, but younger musicians were listening to them for material, and several songs from the Mainer folio were redone in bluegrass style by **the Stanley Brothers**. In his later years, J. E. repaired fiddles, led new Mountaineers on a long series of albums for Rural Rhythm, and corresponded with admirers all over the world.

COMPLIMENTS OF "THE CRAZY COMPANY"
Broadcasting Daily 12:00 Noon over WWNC
(Except Saturday and Sunday)
Also

WWNC Asheville	CRAZY BARN DANCE WBT—Charlotte Every Saturday Night For	WWNC Asheville

CHARLOTTE, N. C.

The original (1935) lineup of Mainer's Mountaineers with program presenter Fisher Hendley (himself a banjoist and country bandleader). With its large cast of well-known artists, the *Crazy Barn Dance* was a considerable rival to the *Grand Ole Opry*.

Instruments: fiddle, harmonica, guitars, vocals
Recording Debut: August 10, 1935

KEY RECORDINGS

Just Because, **1935**
Jolie Blonde, **1936**
Wondering, **1937**
Fais pas ca, **1938**
Une pias ici et une pias la bas, **1938**
She's One of Those, **1938**

Cajun music—the sound of French-speaking southern Louisiana—has a symbiotic relationship with country music. In the '30s, the traditional presentation of Cajun music, by fiddle and diatonic accordion, fell out of favor, and younger musicians drew closer to the sound of the hillbilly stringband, the fiddle now accompanied by guitars and maybe upright bass. The old repertoire, with its piercing cries of loss and guilt, was supplemented by hillbilly songs or mainstream pop, sometimes sung in French, sometimes English.

The most popular Cajun record makers of the '30s were the Hackberry Ramblers, perhaps because their skillful alternation of antique and modern material appealed both to conservative and more broad-minded listeners. The band's founder members were fiddler Luderin Darbone (1913–2008) and singer/guitarists Edwin Duhon (1910–2006), Lennis Sonnier (1917–93), and Floyd Rainwater (1911–60), the last later replaced by Floyd Shreve (1915–57). But their bestselling record was done with singer/guitarist Joe Werner (1909–78), a poignant lost-love song in waltz time called "Wondering."

Darbone swung like the devil in up-tempo numbers such as "Une pias ici et une pias la bas" and "Vinton High Society" and broke hearts on slow ones like "Fais pa ca" (the blues "Trouble in Mind") or the Cajun classic "Jolie Blonde." In just over three years they made more than eighty recordings, generally reserving the Hackberry name for the French releases while issuing the English ones as by the Riverside Ramblers (named after a tire brand advertised on their radio programs). While contemporaries like fiddler Leo Soileau and singer/bandleader "Happy Fats" Broussard were expanding their groups with electric steel guitar and piano, shifting Cajun's center of gravity toward Western Swing, the Hackberry Ramblers preserved the acoustic stringband sound. They went on doing so, with few interruptions, until Darbone's death, seven decades later.

The Hackberry Ramblers at their first recording session, New Orleans, 1935. *From left*: Floyd Rainwater, Luderin Darbone, Lonnie Rainwater, Lennis Sonnier. Hackberry is a small community in Cameron Parish, Louisiana—smaller than it used to be, after repeated batterings by hurricanes in the early 2000s.

DICK HARTMAN'S TENNESSEE RAMBLERS

Instruments: fiddles, harmonica, banjo, guitars, bass, vocals

Recording Debut: January 3, 1935

KEY RECORDINGS

I Got the Carolina Blues, **1935**

Leechburg Polka, **1935**

You've Gotta Eat Your Spinach, Baby [as the Washboard Wonders], **1936**

Give It to Me Daddy [as Hartman's Heart Breakers], **1936**

Don't Put a Tax on the Beautiful Girls [as the Tennessee Ramblers], **1939**

This may not be the best known of '30s hillbilly bands, but they were one of the most versatile. The members were shape-shifters, lining up as Dick Hartman's Tennessee Ramblers, as the Washboard Wonders, and as Hartman's Heart Breakers. The original group had no connection with Tennessee; Hartman (1898–1962) was from West Virginia, and in 1932–33 they played on stations in Pittsburgh and Rochester, New York. They came south in 1934 to join the *Crazy Barn Dance* on WBT in Charlotte. Like that other capable *Barn Dance* combination, **Mainer's Mountaineers**, they drew from every page of the hillbilly playbook: old-time harmony numbers, **Jimmie Rodgers**–style blue yodels, dance music, Hawaiian tunes, hymns. In 1935, it took Bluebird Records two lengthy sessions (forty-two titles) to capture the breadth of their repertoire. Now on WSB in Atlanta, their lineup included fiddler Kenneth "Pappy" Wolfe; Cecil Campbell on banjo, guitar, and Hawaiian guitar; guitarist/singer Harry Blair; Hartman on tenor guitar; and bass player Happy Morris.

The following year, with the Ramblers back on WBT, either Hartman or Bluebird's recording manager Eli Oberstein proposed new iterations of the band. The Washboard Wonders copied the Hoosier Hot Shots, a popular group on WLS in Chicago who jazzed up pop songs with washboard, kazoo, and car horns. Harry Blair's vocals were confidential, like someone leaning in to tell a dirty joke. Hartman's Heart Breakers made a similar novelty-band noise to frame the mock-innocent voice of "Betty Lou" on songs that actually *were* dirty jokes, like "Feels Good" or "Let Me Play with It," now treasured as eye-popping examples of what one could get away with on a '30s hillbilly record.

Blair, Campbell, and fiddler Jack Gillette later featured in a group called the Tennessee Ramblers.

The Tennessee Ramblers, 1935: pioneers of all-American country music, their repertoire embracing "Back to Old Smoky Mountain," "Beautiful Texas," "Melody of Hawaii," and "Pennsylvania Hop."

THREE TOBACCO TAGS

Instruments: mandolins, guitar, vocals
Recording Debut: May 29, 1931

KEY RECORDINGS

V-8 Blues, **1936**
Reno Blues, **1937**
Good Gal Remember Me, **1938**
I Was Only Teasing You, **1938**
Never Was a Married Man, **1938**
When You Go a-Courtin', **1938**

From the mid-'30s, Bluebird Records' twice-yearly visits to Charlotte, North Carolina, to record artists associated with WBT and similar stations built a catalog of Southeastern hillbilly acts as extensive as the one the company was simultaneously creating in Texas with the bands out there, playing what we now call Western Swing (see chapter 4). So is there a case for calling the Tarheel outfits *Eastern* Swing?

It's a tough call. They didn't revere jazz musicians as much as the Southwesterners; they developed steel guitar techniques somewhat differently; they scorned the horn. But some of them did work up a peppy swing music using fiddles and acoustic guitars and mandolins—a sort of bluegrass-in-waiting. One of the most spirited of these groups was the Three Tobacco Tags.

George Wade (1905–58), Luther Baucom (1902–67), and Reid Summey (1903–75) met as millworkers in Gastonia, North Carolina. Their first attempts at recording, in 1931–32, were commercially unsuccessful, but by 1936, with a Bluebird contract and a hit record ("V-8 Blues" and "Courtin'"), they were on their way. They offered a winsome repertoire of blues, heart songs, and slightly naughty comic pieces, with the unique instrumental combination of a guitar and two mandolins.

In 1938, Wade was dropped from the group for rascally behavior, and they became just the Tobacco Tags, since they now numbered four or five, including "Hashhouse" Harvey Ellington on fiddle and mandolin and Sam Pridgin on vocals and bass. They were popular radio personalities on WPTF in Raleigh, North Carolina, and WRVA in Richmond, Virginia, and by the time their Bluebird contract expired in 1941, they had racked up eighty-six recordings. Some of them, like the playful "I Was Only Teasing You," were seized upon decades later and reenergized by bands like the Red Clay Ramblers.

"Tobacco tags" were small, often brightly colored, metal tags identifying brands of chewing tobacco: Red Meat, Brown Mule, Ida May, and hundreds more.

BLUE SKY BOYS

Dates: Bill Bolick, b. October 28, 1917, East Hickory, NC; d. March 13, 2008, Hickory, NC
Earl Bolick, b. November 16, 1919, East Hickory, NC; d. April 19, 1998, Suwanee, GA
Instruments: mandolin, guitar, vocals
Recording Debut: June 16, 1936

KEY RECORDINGS

Sunny Side of Life, **1936**
Down on the Banks of the Ohio, **1936**
Story of the Knoxville Girl, **1937**
Are You from Dixie?, **1939**
Turn Your Radio On, **1940**

One of the most beautiful and distinctive sounds in country music is the close harmony of the Blue Sky Boys: silken duets, with Earl Bolick taking the lead and his brother Bill the tenor part, delicately underpinned by Bill's mandolin and Earl's guitar. They began singing on radio in their teens, first on WWNC in Asheville, then on WGST in Atlanta, where their audience appeal led to them being signed to Bluebird Records, for whom they made almost a hundred recordings in the second half of the '30s. Their repertoire—perhaps modeled to some extent on that of **the Carter Family**, from whom they got favorite pieces like "Sunny Side of Life"—embraced songs of love, loss, old-time religion, and long-ago murders, as in "Story of the Knoxville Girl" and "Down on the Banks of the Ohio." "Are You from Dixie?," their theme song, was atypically lighthearted, but, unlike contemporaries such as **the Delmore Brothers** or **Three Tobacco Tags**, they seldom picked comic songs and always steered well clear of the blues.

They maintained their radio presence and recording contracts for a few years after World War II, working on a succession of Southern stations, but a gap was opening up between their sober, god-fearing songs and the more lurid repertoire of honky-tonk. They quit the music business in 1951, but in the '60s, thanks to their admirers, they were engaged to play at college folk clubs and folk festivals, and they made several albums, sounding hardly different from their twenty-something selves. But though the closeness of their singing was unimpaired, their personal relationship was unharmonious, and attempts to reunite them repeatedly failed. Their legacy lies in the sound of **the Louvin Brothers** and the Everly Brothers, and in the many pieces they circulated that have entered the bluegrass songbook.

"On the Old Plantation" (1937) was one of many compositions about slavery days ("The Little Old Log Cabin in the Lane," "Take Me Back to the Sweet Sunny South," and so on) that passed into the repertoires of early country singers.

THE DEZURIK SISTERS

Dates: Mary Jane DeZurik, b. February 1, 1917, Royalton, MN; d. September 3, 1981, Melrose Park, IL
Caroline DeZurik, b. December 24, 1918, Royalton, MN; d. April 16, 2009, West Chicago, IL
Instruments: guitar (Mary Jane), vocals
Recording Debut: December 16, 1938

KEY RECORDINGS

Sweet Hawaiian Chimes, **1938**
Guitar Blues, **1938**
The Arizona Yodeler, **1938**

If yodeling strikes you as an odd concept, the DeZurik Sisters will seem to come from somewhere beyond the surreal. When they unite their pretty, bell-clear voices in harmonized yodels, they sound like nightingales on helium. But their work goes further, creating audio pictures of the farmyard, with its bleating lambs, cooing doves, and chuckling chickens. Not content to imitate livestock, they replicate musical instruments—tinkling mandolins, wah-wah trumpets, whining Hawaiian guitars.

The DeZuriks came from central Minnesota, growing up surrounded by the farm animals whose sounds they would one day transform. As teenagers, they were spotted performing at a county fair by a representative of the WLS Artists' Bureau, and soon they were on the *National Barn Dance*, broadcasting to millions of people like themselves in rural Midwestern communities. The animal-feed manufacturer Purina heard one of their specialty chicken yodels and signed them to its stage and radio show, *Checkerboard Time*, billing them as the Cackle Sisters. Though they made a few regular recordings in 1938, the DeZuriks were more widely known from their transcription programs, heard on radio stations across most of the United States.

In 1944, after a spell on a barn dance program in St. Paul, Minnesota, they took the Purina dollar again, now engaged in touring with **Eddy Arnold** and appearing on the *Grand Ole Opry*. Transcriptions from this time give us the full flavor of the sisters' farmyard fantasias. Mary Jane retired in 1947 and was replaced by their sister Lorraine (1926–2009). She and Caroline subsequently jumped genre, repositioning themselves in polka music. In 1951, Caroline took the role, once held by **Patsy Montana**, of featured singer with the Prairie Ramblers, and in later years, she was known as the advertising voice of Busch beer.

The WLS Family Album for 1940 introduces its readers to one of the station's most popular acts. When the sisters first joined the *Barn Dance*, listeners wrote in to enthuse about them. "The best singers and yodelers I have ever heard," said one fan. "I'd sit up all night to hear them."

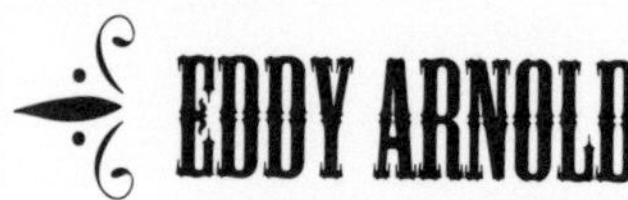

EDDY ARNOLD

Dates: Richard Edward Arnold, b. May 15, 1918, Henderson, TN; d. May 8, 2008, Nashville, TN
Instruments: guitar, vocals
Recording Debut: 1945

KEY RECORDINGS

That's How Much I Love You, **1946**
Bouquet of Roses, **1948**
The Cattle Call, **1955**
What's He Doing in My World, **1965**
Make the World Go Away, **1965**

Arnold brought a new sound to country music in the '40s and '50s: a warm, buffed vocal manner, pitched between the smooth country style of Gene Autry or Jimmie Davis and the crooning of Bing Crosby or Perry Como. Country music historian Bill C. Malone called Arnold's approach "as appealing to bankers as to farmers."

Arnold grew up on a farm, learned guitar, and, at eighteen, made his radio debut on WTJS in Jackson, Tennessee; within a few years, he was a regular on WMPS in Memphis. During World War II, he joined the *Camel Caravan*, a country troupe, sponsored by the R. J. Reynolds cigarette company, that toured service bases. With energetic promotion by his manager, "Colonel" Tom Parker (before he filled that role for Elvis Presley), Arnold signed with RCA Victor and was soon scoring hits; he had five country chart-toppers in 1948. Over the next two decades, he was one of country music's most bankable recording artists. A cast member of the *Grand Ole Opry*, he also appeared on network radio and TV shows, had his own TV series, and even guest-hosted *The Tonight Show Starring Johnny Carson*.

For some country music lovers, this success came at a cost: It wasn't just Arnold's singing and dapper stage wear that were overstepping the boundaries of genre, but the musical settings of records like "Cattle Call," accompanied by the Hugo Winterhalter Orchestra. Arnold dismissed such carping. As he saw it, country music needed to "cut out the by-cracky nonsense"—the bib-and-brace overalls, the yodeling, the cornball humor. His stylistic followers were similarly ingratiating crossover artists like Jim Reeves and Kenny Rogers. His 1966 elevation to the Country Music Hall of Fame caused controversy, but his admirers point to the figures: Over six decades, he sold more than eighty million records.

Eddy Arnold emerges from his hit-decorated trailer. His revival of "Anytime," a pop song from the 1920s, topped *Billboard*'s "Juke Box Folk Records"—an early country chart—in 1948.

Recorded by GENE AUTRY on Columbia Record

COWBOY & WESTERN MUSIC

The Old West, the frontier days: these foundational images—half hard fact, half malleable myth—have sunk deep into the American psyche and can be recalled in a moment by a movie or a lyric. Songs of cowboy life, some once sung by actual cowboys, were popularized on records from the mid-1920s onward, but as the days of the cattle drives slipped further and further into history, songwriters turned to creating an imaginary West full of adventure, romance, and rhythm—a territory whose genial rangers were **Gene Autry, Tex Ritter**, and the **Sons of the Pioneers**.

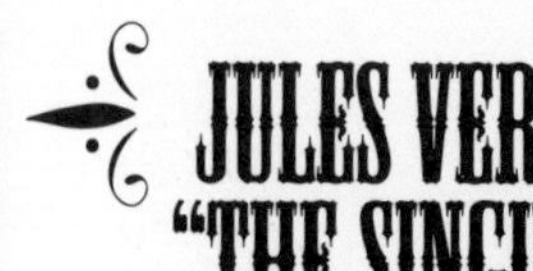

JULES VERNE ALLEN, "THE SINGING COWBOY"

Dates: b. April 1, 1883, Waxahachie, TX; d. March 19, 1942, Tucson, AZ
Instruments: guitar, vocals
Recording Debut: April 21, 1928

KEY RECORDINGS

Little Joe, the Wrangler, **1928**
Jack o' Diamonds, **1928**
The Days of Forty-Nine, **1928**
Home on the Range, **1928**
Chisholm Trail, **1929**
Cowboy's Lament [a.k.a. Streets of Laredo], **1929**

At the end of the 1920s, a middle-aged Texan with the somewhat exotic name of Jules Verne Allen recorded more than a score of songs sung by cowboys. In a wind-dried voice, to the accompaniment of a jog-along guitar and sometimes a fiddle or a harmonica, he recounted tales like "The Days of Forty-Nine," "Home on the Range," and "When the Work's All Done This Fall." "Old songs of the trail," a reviewer called them, "that have been sung around a thousand campfires in the days of the Old West."

Allen claimed to know what he was singing about: In his youth, he had worked on ranches and trail drives all over the Southwest. (He had also been a deputy sheriff and border patrolman in Texas and spent a couple of years in the US Army.) He learned to play guitar while recovering from an encounter with a bad-tempered bronc and began performing onstage—including the Deadwood stage—at variety theaters and honky-tonks. By the late 1920s, now based in Albuquerque, New Mexico, he was a star of *The First American*, an annual pageant devoted to the history, music, and folkways of Native Americans. In 1929, the governor made him the state's official cowboy singer.

His recording career, though productive, lasted little more than a year, but he was already an experienced broadcaster. In the early '30s, in San Antonio, he fronted "Longhorn Luke & His Cowboys," described in a local paper as "an amusing program of plains ballads and colossal lies." He also gave talks, interspersed with songs, about cowboy life and its ways, and in 1933 published a book on the subject, including three dozen of his songs. *Cowboy Lore* was praised by *Time* magazine and the *New York Times* and remained in print for many years.

Cowboy Lore, said the *New York Times* in June 1933, "adds first-hand picturesque knowledge to the store of information that is slowly being gathered to preserve and commemorate the epoch of the cattle range in American history."

HARRY "MAC" McCLINTOCK

Dates: Harry K. McClintock, b. October 8, 1882, Knoxville, TN; d. April 24, 1957, San Francisco, CA
Instruments: guitar, vocals
Recording Debut: March 1, 1928

KEY RECORDINGS

The Bum Song, **1928, 1938**
The Old Chisholm Trail, **1928**
The Trail to Mexico, **1928**
Hallelujah! I'm a Bum, **1928, 1938**
The Big Rock Candy Mountains, **1928, 1938**

Many old-time country artists are remembered for a single song or tune, but Harry McClintock boasts two: "The Big Rock Candy Mountains" and "Hallelujah! I'm a Bum," both of which he claimed he wrote. The first is a tramp's dream of a place *"where the handouts grow on bushes, and you sleep out every night . . . the boxcars all are empty and the sun shines every day."* "Hallelujah!," based on an old hymn, "Revive Us Again," was a down-to-earth evocation of the hobo life: *"I went to a house, and I rapped on the door / The lady says, 'Bum, bum, you've been here before.'"* In an era of lost jobs and deserted homes, these half-comic, half-documentary songs of all-American economic migrants had a real grip on the national imagination.

"Mac," as he called himself professionally, knew about vagrancy from way back, having been a freight-train-hopping hobo since his teens. Around the turn of the last century, he went to sea, working on ships that took him to the Philippines, China, Africa, Australia, and England. Returning to the United States, he became a railroader and joined the "One Big Union," the Industrial Workers of the World, which later adopted "Hallelujah!" as its unofficial anthem. In the 1920s, settled in San Francisco, he led his "Haywire Orchestry" on radio station KFRC, singing, in a good-humored, faintly Irish American brogue, cowboy songs like "The Old Chisholm Trail" and "Goodbye, Old Paint," many of which he recorded. He continued broadcasting until the '50s, also appearing in movies and on TV. More than forty years after his death, he was in a movie again, or his voice was—chanting "The Big Rock Candy Mountains" over the opening credits of another Depression-era fantasy, the Coen brothers' *O Brother, Where Art Thou?*

"Haywire Mac" (*seated, front and center*) and his troupe dispensed clean Western fun over the San Francisco airwaves.

THE BEVERLY HILL BILLIES

Instruments: fiddles, accordion, guitars, string bass, vocals
Recording Debut: April 25, 1930

KEY RECORDINGS

When the Bloom Is on the Sage, **1930**
Red River Valley, **1930**
The Strawberry Roan, **1931**
The Big Corral, **1932**
Cowboy Joe, **1932**

In the spring of 1930, ads began to appear in the Southern California press for a new act on KMPC Berkeley: "Hey! Hey! H'yah they come! Fresh from them thar mountings—The Beverly Hill-Billies," offering "The Songs Your Dad and Mother Sang" for an hour every night except Monday. By late summer, they were appearing regularly at Grauman's Chinese Theater: "Mister Tall Feller (Glen Rice) . . . introduces them . . . Ezra [Paulette] sings and plays the violin, Lem [Giles, a.k.a. Aleth Hansen] handles the guitar, Dave [possibly Jad Dees] yodels with his guitar, Hank [Skillet, a.k.a. Harry Blaeholder] manipulates a violin and Zeke [Manners] plays the concertina [actually, accordion]."

Rice, KMPC's station manager and announcer, claimed he had discovered the group "living in the hills of Beverly" and persuaded them to "ride down from the hill-top habitats on horses and mules every evening." He expanded this fanciful backstory to embrace the teenage singer and yodeler **Elton Britt**.

The group's "old-time songs of a half-forgotten era," said one journalist, "afford a pleasant relief from the ear-splitting productions of the average jazz orchestra." At that time, nervous listeners were often comforted in such terms. Similar reassurances decorate the press releases of a contemporary group, the Blue Ridge Ramblers, who were introducing hillbilly music to the Eastern Seaboard much as the Beverly Hill Billies were to Angelenos.

By the mid-'30s, more ear-catching competitors like **the Sons of the Pioneers** were jostling the Hill Billies aside, though they carried on recording in various combinations until 1937. Their name lives on (thanks to oldies channels) in the much-loved TV sitcom *The Beverly Hillbillies* (1962–71), about an overnight-rich Ozark family who migrate to the Hills. The original Hill Billies sued the producers for infringement of their name and won a settlement.

Western groups like the Beverly Hill Billies, their songs packed with the evocative topography of prairies and peaks, created an idea of "country and western" music that in faraway lands like Australia and the United Kingdom would hold sway for decades.

GENE AUTRY

Dates: Orvon Grover Autry, b. September 29, 1907, Tioga, TX; d. October 2, 1998, Studio City, CA
Instruments: guitar, vocals
Recording Debut: October 9, 1929

KEY RECORDINGS

Cowboy('s) Yodel, **1929–30**
That's How I Got My Start, **1931**
Silver Haired Daddy of Mine [with Jimmy Long], **1931**
The Yellow Rose of Texas, **1933**
Back in the Saddle Again, **1939**

He was a fixture in almost a hundred Western movies as "The Singing Cowboy." A rodeo entrepreneur, real-estate tycoon, TV star, and media mogul. A perennial voice of Christmastide, thanks to his recording of "Rudolph, the Red-Nosed Reindeer." But beyond these high points of Gene Autry's career lie the no-less-colorful foothills of his early years. Inspired, like many of his generation, by **Jimmie Rodgers**, he became an expert imitator, both vocally and with guitar, practicing, so the story goes, during slow times while working as a telegraph operator in Oklahoma. Making his way to New York, he was engaged by record companies to replicate the Blue Yodeler's songs, or at least mimic his style. Sometimes, he went a little further than Rodgers might have ventured, as in the suggestive "Rheumatism Blues" and "Black Bottom Blues." For much of 1929–32, this was Autry's primary job in the recording studio. (On radio, he could be more independent.)

Rodgers's death in 1933—which Autry of course commemorated, on records like "The Life of Jimmie Rodgers"—freed him from his role as a copyist, but he had already begun to blaze his own trail with the enormously successful "Silver Haired Daddy of Mine," a duet with his sidekick Jimmy Long (1889–1953). Through the '30s, he purveyed romance, nostalgia, and, as his B-movie career burgeoned, the Old West. The sound of his records in the late '30s and early '40s—accompanied by fiddlers Carl Cotner and **Spade Cooley**, steel guitarist Frankie Marvin, and piano accordionist Paul Sells—was full of the lush Western warmth of Hollywood. Coloring the work of contemporaries like **Jimmie Davis** and **the Sons Of The Pioneers**, it became practically a default mode of Western-leaning country music until well into the '50s.

Gene Autry toured the USA incessantly during the '30s and '40s, often with sidekicks like comedian Smilie Burnette and steel guitarist Frankie Marvin.

JIMMIE DAVIS

Dates: James Houston Davis, b. September 11, 1899, Bienville Parish, LA; d. November 5, 2000, Shreveport, LA
Instruments: guitar, vocals
Recording Debut: July/August 1928

KEY RECORDINGS

She's a Hum Dum Dinger from Dingersville, **1930**
Where the Old Red River Flows, **1930**, **1962**
Nobody's Darling but Mine, **1934**, **1937**
It Makes No Difference Now, **1939**
You Are My Sunshine, **1940**

Jimmie Davis should be remembered as long as people sing "You Are My Sunshine," a standard for more than eighty years (and, it's said, the favorite song of Winston Churchill). Its glow has cast into shadow a period of his career when he specialized in rather different material—songs like "Jelly Roll Blues" or "Tom Cat and Pussy Blues."

In his twenties, Davis taught at Dodd College in Shreveport and had a program on the local station KWKH. Between 1929 and 1933, he recorded busily for Victor, following the example of the label's star, **Jimmie Rodgers**, by developing a portfolio of mother-and-home songs, cowboy tales, comic narratives, and suggestive—sometimes *very* suggestive—blues. Whatever the theme, it was gracefully sung, usually with a yodel, and occasionally accompanied, as on "She's a Hum Dum Dinger from Dingersville," by the (uncredited) African American guitarists Ed Schaffer and Oscar Woods. In 1934, having moved to Decca, he recorded "Nobody's Darling but Mine," a hit covered by Bing Crosby. His songbook now almost blues-free, he expanded it with compositions by other musicians (Floyd Tillman, **Bill Nettles**, **Buddy Jones**, and others) in which, as with "Sunshine," he acquired partial or total publishing rights.

A country music star almost ranking alongside **Gene Autry**, Davis used his fame to underwrite campaigns for public office, first as Shreveport's commissioner for public safety, then as state governor, when his stump speeches would segue into stringband music. While on the campaign trail, he hired excellent players from the Texas swing bands, such as pianist **Moon Mullican** and fiddler **Cliff Bruner**. He maintained his music career through two terms in the governor's mansion (1944–48 and 1960–64) and remained on Decca's roster into the '70s. In his later years, he concentrated on gospel music and his now extensive publishing interests.

Davis claimed he wrote "Nobody's Darlin' but Mine" as a young man, but more likely he acquired it, like other songs to which he put his name, with a one-off payment to a penurious songwriter.

THE SONS OF THE PIONEERS

Instruments: fiddle, guitars, bass, vocals
Recording Debut: August 8, 1934

KEY RECORDINGS
'Way Out There, **1934, 1937**
Tumbling Tumbleweeds, **1934, 1937**
Roving Cowboy, **1935**
Empty Saddles, **1936**
So Long to the Red River Valley, **1941**
Cool Water, **1941**

In the early '30s, Southern California, already the home of the Western movie, became the radio and recording center for Western music. **The Beverly Hill Billies** and Stuart Hamblen's Covered Wagon Jubilee injected ingenuity and pep into the myths of the range and the Rockies, and the stories of the cowboys and cowgirls who, at least in imagination, still populated them. But a new group of musicians were coming to town whose wide-screen Technicolor depictions of the Old West would make their predecessors' efforts look like black-and-white antiques from the silent era.

The original Sons of the Pioneers were Len Slye (later known as **Roy Rogers**), Tim Spencer (1908–74), and Bob Nolan (1908–80). Nolan possessed not only a handsome voice but a rare gift of capturing the colors and moods of the Western landscape in unforgettable phrases and heart-turning melodies, such as "Tumbling Tumbleweeds," which became the group's theme song.

New members quickly joined: the fiddler Hugh Farr (famously praised for the excellence of his bowing by the conductor Leopold Stokowski), then his brother Karl Marx Farr, a guitarist of extraordinary technique and imagination. The Stéphane Grappelli and Django Reinhardt of country music, their instrumental duets were showcased in the group's many radio transcriptions.

The Sons' faultless close harmony, also heard on Decca recordings and in Western B movies, provided a model no singing group could ignore, and their influence swept across hillbilly music, both Western and Eastern. Singer/guitarist Lloyd Perryman (1917–77) joined them in 1936, and the following year bass player Pat Brady (1914–72) replaced Slye/Rogers. The Sons remained the ranch bosses of Western music until 1949, when Nolan and Spencer retired. But this was not the end: Groupings of veterans and new members would keep the sound of the Sons alive for several more decades.

Published in New York from 1944 to 1947 or later, *The Mountain Broadcast and Prairie Recorder* was one of the earliest country music fanzines.

TEX RITTER

Dates: Woodward Maurice Ritter, b. January 12, 1905, Murvaul, TX; d. January 2, 1974, Nashville, TN
Instruments: guitar, vocals
Recording Debut: September 2, 1933

KEY RECORDINGS

Good-Bye, Old Paint, **1933**
Rye Whiskey, Rye Whiskey, **1933**
I'm Wastin' My Tears on You, **1944**
The Deck of Cards, **1948**
The Ballad of High Noon (Do Not Forsake Me, Oh My Darlin'), **1952**

Ritter's great brown bear of a voice has become familiar to generations of movie fans, notably setting the scene for the climax of *High Noon* (1952). By then, he had been unfolding Western tales for twenty years with the knowledge and authority of a history professor, but with a quite unacademic vigor and humor.

In 1931, as a young actor making his way in New York, Ritter had appeared in the play *Green Grow the Lilacs* and delivered a cowboy song or two. This probably led to his first recordings, "Good-Bye, Old Paint" (a cowboy's farewell to his horse) and "Rye Whiskey, Rye Whiskey," a disc that found buyers as far away as the UK and Australia. Through kids' radio shows like *The Lone Star Rangers* and *Cowboy Tom's Roundup*, and with his records of range life such as "Out on the Lone Prairie," "Hittin' the Trail," and "Singin' in the Saddle," he became, both for children and adults, one of the nation's best-known storytellers of the West. Meanwhile, his prolific moviemaking—he appeared in sixty cinematic horse operas between 1936 and 1945—ensured that he was also one of the West's most recognizable figures. For a generation, maybe two, Tex Ritter was the John Wayne of cowboy music.

But he was not corralled by it: In 1944, as one of the first artists to sign with the new indie label Capitol, he placed "I'm Wastin' My Tears on You" on both country and pop charts. In the '60s, based in Nashville and a member of the *Grand Ole Opry*, he used his status as a Grand Old Man of Western Music to help create the Country Music Association and the Country Music Hall of Fame. Like fellow *Opry* stalwart **Roy Acuff**, he stood, unsuccessfully, for office on the Republican ticket.

Throughout the '50s and '60s, Tex Ritter maintained a busy schedule of appearances at rodeos, state fairs, and, evidently, shopping malls. Hank Morton was his in-house comedian.

ELTON BRITT

Dates: James Elton Britt Baker, b. June 27, 1913, Searcy County, AR; d. June 22, 1972, Connellsville, PA
Instruments: guitar, vocals
Recording Debut: August 8, 1933

KEY RECORDINGS

Alpine Milkman Yodel, **1933**
Chime Bells, **1934, 1939**
There's a Star Spangled Banner Waving Somewhere, **1942**
Someday (You'll Want Me to Want You), **1945**

Elton Britt broke into the country music recording scene in 1933, when he and an older brother, Vern, made a slew of widely marketed discs for ARC under the billing "Wenatchee Mountaineers." They deftly presented themselves, with the kind of versatility the new industry approved of, as equally capable of delivering Western songs and foot-tapping fiddle tunes. Elton was also an accomplished yodeler—not in the blue-yodel idiom of **Jimmie Rodgers**, but in the prettier, more precise, and more technically challenging style of the Alpine yodelers who had long been a staple of American vaudeville, as he demonstrated in "Swiss Yodel" and "Alpine Milkman Yodel." Earlier, he had worked in Los Angeles with **the Beverly Hill Billies**—recommended by fellow Searcy County musician Hubert (Hugh) Ashley, who had had Elton's brothers Vern and Arle in his Melody Makers stringband—and he recombined with some of them under the rube billing of "Pappy, Ezra, Zeke, and Elton" before going solo in 1936.

Three years later, a second recording of Britt's yodeling showpiece "Chime Bells" initiated his career on his new label, Bluebird, where he furthered his association with the songwriter, producer, and publisher **Bob Miller**. Soon after the United States entered World War II, Miller gave Britt a patriotic number he had just acquired, "There's a Star Spangled Banner Waving Somewhere." It was an immediate hit, even making it into *Billboard*'s pop Top Ten, and was quickly reissued on a War Department–sponsored "V-Disc" for distribution to US military bases. It also became the song by which Britt would be best remembered, though he continued to make records, sometimes dueting with the cowgirl singer Rosalie Allen, and movies (such as *Laramie* in 1949), and to feature in radio and TV broadcasts of the *Grand Ole Opry* and the WWVA *Jamboree*.

Elton Britt's career hit "There's a Star Spangled Banner Waving Somewhere" was the first country recording to be awarded a gold disc.

ROY ROGERS

Dates: Leonard Franklin Slye, b. November 5, 1911, Cincinnati, OH; d. July 6, 1998, Apple Valley, CA
Instruments: guitar, vocals
Recording Debut: August 8, 1934 [with the Sons of the Pioneers]

KEY RECORDINGS

Hadie Brown, **1937**
Listen to the Rhythm of the Range, **1938**
There's a Ranch in the Rockies, **1938**
Don't Fence Me In, **1944**
Blue Shadows on the Trail [with the SOTP], **1948**

When they buried Roy Rogers, they might have kept the spades for another task: clearing away the layers of his legend—the B movies, the restaurant franchise, the jokes about his horse, Trigger—and digging down to his legacy to country music, as a founder of **the Sons of the Pioneers** and singer of songs evoking the grandeur and freedom of the mountains and prairies, the new Eden of the Old West.

He grew up in rural Ohio, a musically talented kid named Leonard Slye. In 1930, the Slyes moved to Los Angeles, where Len worked on radio with the Rocky Mountaineers, day-jobbing as a peach picker for Del Monte. Listeners were slow to say, "Yes!," and for several years he sang in short-lived groups with friends like Bob Nolan and Tim Spencer, culminating in the Pioneer Trio and finally the Sons of the Pioneers.

In 1937, now Roy Rogers, he replaced **Gene Autry** as Republic Pictures' new Western star. Recording in his new name, he mixed swing numbers with Western landscape songs such as the gorgeous "Don't Fence Me In," which added the wit of Cole Porter to the sunny delivery of the man whom moviegoers called "King of the Cowboys."

He still worked with the Pioneers on movies and discs, but in the '50s and '60s he was mostly elsewhere, making movies; hosting a TV show with his partner, Dale Evans (whom he married in 1947), and Trigger; and building a business empire. Given what another movie actor would later achieve, he could probably have stood successfully for public office. One can guess his ticket: Rogers was nothing if not a clean-living, conservative American.

"What's the matter with you? Don't you like girls?" Bob Hope asks him in the movie *Son of Paleface*.

"I'll stick to horses, mister," Roy replies.

Roy Rogers sings for children at a rally held by the evangelist Billy Graham in Harringay, north London, March 1954.

REX ALLEN

Dates: Rex Elvie Allen Sr., b. December 31, 1920, Cochise County, AZ; d. December 17, 1999, Tucson, AZ
Instruments: guitar, vocals
Recording Debut: 1949

KEY RECORDINGS

The Arizona Waltz, **1950**
Crying in the Chapel, **1953**
Teardrops in My Heart, **1958**
Don't Go Near the Indians, **1961**

According to Western music historian Doug Green, Rex Allen "was the last of the singing cowboys. The last signed; the last to make a singing-cowboy Western, *The Phantom Stallion*, in 1954." His strong, velvet voice was first heard on the radio in 1944–45 from stations in Trenton, New Jersey, and Philadelphia; he then leaped from these modest beginnings to the cast of the WLS *National Barn Dance*. (According to one account, he had first auditioned for the *Grand Ole Opry* but lost out to Eddy Arnold.) Spotted by Republic Pictures, he made almost a score of Western movies, starting with *The Arizona Cowboy* in 1949. He recorded prolifically for Mercury and Decca, and his 1958 album *Under Western Skies* remained in catalog for many years.

When the musical Western faded from the nation's screens, Allen moved to television, acting in *Frontier Doctor* and appearing on country music showcases like *Town Hall Party* and his own *Rex Allen Show*. For Disney Studios, he narrated documentaries and children's films, including an animated version of E. B. White's *Charlotte's Web*. His burnished voice was also heard in many TV ads.

A popular figure on the rodeo circuit, he was elected Rodeo Man of the Year in 1965. He had been an accomplished bronc rider in his teens, and it had been a close choice between singing and a rodeo career. "I love the personal appearances of a rodeo or county fair," he said, "more than anything else in my life." He was voted into the Cowboy Hall of Fame and helped found the Western Music Association. He gave his son, Rex Allen Jr., a start in country music, and in 1995 they collaborated on the album *The Singing Cowboys*. For many years, Willcox, Arizona, commemorated him with an annual Rex Allen Day.

In *Old Oklahoma Plains* (1952), Rex Allen takes time off from rodeo riding to settle a land dispute.

WESTERN SWING

The young musicians joining or forming bands in the Southwest in the early '30s were not like their predecessors. This new generation had grown up to the sounds and rhythms of ragtime, jazz, and blues. They were intrigued by the notion of incorporating them—and the novel technology of instrumental amplification—into their inherited vocabulary of stringband hoedown music. The result of this experiment would be called Western Swing. It would revolutionize both the makeup of the country band and the orchestration of country music—producing, along the way, such expansive personalities as **Bob Wills, Milton Brown,** and **Spade Cooley.**

THE LIGHT CRUST DOUGHBOYS

Instruments: fiddles, steel guitar, accordion, piano, guitars, tenor banjo, bass, vocals
Recording Debut: February 9, 1932 [as Fort Worth Doughboys]

KEY RECORDINGS

Nancy Jane [as FWD], **1932**
The Eyes of Texas, **1937**
Gin Mill Blues, **1938**
Pussy, Pussy, Pussy, **1938**
Mama Won't Let Me, **1939**
Beer Drinkin' Mama, **1939**

The first Western Swing record (though no one called it that at the time) was made in 1932 by **Bob Wills** (fiddle), **Milton Brown** (vocal), and Derwood Brown and "Sleepy" Johnson (guitars). They were the house band of the Burrus Mill & Elevator Company of Fort Worth, manufacturers of Light Crust flour, but Victor Records, perhaps unwilling to do the company's advertising for them, hid the brand name by calling the group the Fort Worth Doughboys. It hardly mattered; within a year or so, the musicians had scattered, to be replaced by long-stayers like fiddler Clifford Gross, singer Leon Huff, and guitarist Ramon DeArman, while their manager/promoter, W. Lee O'Daniel, looked for a less fussy record label. He found one in Brunswick's Vocalion marque, and the records the band began making in 1933 were credited to the Light Crust Doughboys.

That 1932 disc—coupling an effervescent pop song, "Sunbonnet Sue," with "Nancy Jane," a good-time hokum blues from the "race" catalog—epitomized the mixed lineage of Western Swing. The Doughboys expanded the baggy definition to bursting point, slotting the small-group jazz of "Gin Mill Blues" or "Blue Guitars" (featuring newer members like pianist Knocky Parker, electric guitarist Muryel Campbell, and banjoist Marvin Montgomery) alongside the polka "We Must Have Beer," cowboy songs like "Cattle Call," and pop nonsense such as "I Like Bananas Because They Have No Bones." A jukebox favorite was the insouciant "Pussy, Pussy, Pussy," supposedly about a shrill-voiced woman calling out to her cat. The Doughboys made more records than Wills, but their sessions were just pit stops in years of grueling tours, playing in the street outside Light Crust retailers, making remote broadcasts, and ending the day with a four-hour dance. Montgomery kept the band going after World War II, recording for King and hanging on into the LP era.

Above: A 1932 lineup of the Light Crust Doughboys, featuring Herman Arnspiger (guitar), Bob Wills (fiddle), singer Milton Brown, and Burrus Mills honcho W. Lee O'Daniel. *Right*: Different Doughboys in disguise, a few years later.

MILTON BROWN

Dates: b. September 8, 1903, Stephenville, TX; d. April 18, 1936, Fort Worth, TX
Instrument: vocals
Recording Debut: [as leader] April 4, 1934

KEY RECORDINGS

Just Sitting on Top of the World, **1934**
Chinatown, My Chinatown, **1935**
My Mary, **1935**
Stay on the Right Side Sister, **1936**
Texas Hambone Blues, **1936**
Somebody Stole My Gal, **1936**
Yes Sir!, **1936**

When Milton Brown left **the Light Crust Doughboys** in 1932, he formed a band of his own, the Musical Brownies, and for the next four years played most weekends at the Crystal Springs Dance Pavilion in Fort Worth. Originally a conventional fiddle-fronted stringband like the Doughboys, the Brownies began to lean jazzward when they hired pianist Fred Calhoun. According to his younger brother Roy Lee Brown, Milton created a series of firsts: "The first [Western Swing band] to have a jazz piano, the first to have double fiddles, the first to use amplified instruments."

The Brownies recorded in 1934 for Bluebird and in January 1935 for Decca, stacking up more than fifty recordings before **Bob Wills**'s Texas Playboys ever entered a studio. Milton's singing combined the neighborly warmth of Bing Crosby with the preacher-on-a-roll fervor of jazz vocalists like Cab Calloway, and he could switch from a contemporary pop song like "Love in Bloom" to the college chant "The Eyes of Texas" to a riotous "Garbage Man Blues" ("*Stick out your can, here comes the garbage man!*"). In 1936, equipped with the fiddling team of Cecil Brower and **Cliff Bruner** and the revolutionary electric steel guitarist **Bob Dunn**, the Brownies were the hottest thing in Western Swing.

And then it all fell apart. Driving back to town from a gig, Milton crashed his automobile; he died in a hospital a couple of days later. His younger brother Derwood, the band's guitarist and occasional singer, kept it going for a couple of years and another recording session, but before then, key members like Bruner and Dunn had quit to form their own groups, to be followed by banjoist Ocie Stockard. These spin-offs maintained the lively spirit of the original band, but there was no replacing the voice that had been its heart.

The Brownies on the air, ca. 1935. *From left*: Wanna Coffman (bass), an unidentified announcer, Milton Brown, Jesse Ashlock (fiddle), Fred "Papa" Calhoun (piano), Cecil Brower (fiddle), Ocie Stockard (tenor banjo), Derwood Brown (guitar).

BOB WILLS

Dates: James Robert Wills, b. March 6, 1905, Kosse, TX; d. May 13, 1975, Fort Worth, TX
Instruments: fiddle, vocals
Recording Debut: [as leader] September 23, 1935

KEY RECORDINGS

Steel Guitar Rag, **1936**
White Heat, **1937**
That's What I Like About the South, **1938**
Time Changes Everything, **1940**
New San Antonio Rose, **1940**
Twin Guitar Special, **1941**
Take Me Back to Tulsa, **1941**

When, like **Milton Brown**, he broke away from **the Light Crust Doughboys**, Bob Wills put together a band called the Texas Playboys, only to quit Texas for Tulsa, Oklahoma, where he played at Cain's Dancing Academy and broadcast daily on KVOO—often remotely, since he and his band were constantly on the road for their sponsor, Playboy Flour. Wills's Vocalion recordings exhibit all the threads in the fabric of Western Swing: blues derived from the "race" catalogs, like their first hit, "Swing Blues #1"; **Jimmie Rodgers** songs; instrumental stomps; 1920s popular songs; echoes of Mexico and Hawaii.

Wills saw the Western Swing combo not as a stringband but as an orchestra, up to seventeen strong, with brass, reeds, and drums. "New San Antonio Rose," sung by Tommy Duncan, a Western Bing Crosby, was like a manifesto: no fiddles or steel guitar but mariachi-style brass and reeds. Wills's perceived rivals were not hillbilly groups but the swing bands of Benny Goodman, Tommy Dorsey, and Woody Herman, and when, during World War II, he relocated to California, to play in huge ballrooms for war-industry workers, it was those bandleaders' audiences he took pride in matching—and often beating.

Somewhat constrained on records by the requirements of jukebox operators, the Playboys flowered in the mid-'40s when making prerecorded radio programs. Accomplished musicians like fiddlers Louis Tierney and Joe Holley, electric guitarist "Junior" Barnard, mandolinist Tiny Moore, and steel players Herb Remington and Noel Boggs played jazz and blues with skill, originality, and panache.

Big bands became economically unfeasible after the war, but Wills hung on—if not in great shape—until, in the '70s, country stars like Merle Haggard and Waylon Jennings acknowledged their love of Western Swing, and the music enjoyed a revival. In 1974, Haggard produced Wills's farewell album, *For the Last Time*.

Rhythm Round-Up (1945) included the popular novelty group the Hoosier Hotshots as well as the Texas Playboys, featuring singer Tommy Duncan (*second from left*) and Bob Wills (*fourth from left*).

BILL BOYD & HIS COWBOY RAMBLERS

Instruments: fiddles, clarinet, steel guitar, piano, banjo, guitars, bass, vocals
Recording Debut: August 7, 1934

KEY RECORDINGS

The Train Song, **1935**
Under the Double Eagle, **1935**
Wah Hoo, **1936**
Way Out There, **1936**
You Shall Be Free Monah, **1936**
New Steel Guitar Rag, **1937**
Spanish Fandango, **1938**

Fans of **Bob Wills** and **Milton Brown** duke it out over who is the king and who is the father of Western Swing, but you hear less about the runners-up in this league, such as the Hi-Flyers, the Tune Wranglers, or Bill Boyd's Cowboy Ramblers. True, none of them had a front man with the charisma of Wills or Brown, but to the proprietors of dancehalls and the stockists of tavern jukeboxes, they were major players. Bill Boyd (1910–77) made nearly 180 Bluebird recordings in the seven years leading up to World War II (and more afterward), ranging from Western songs to old-time hoedown numbers to hillbilly jazz. He preferred the cowboy repertoire he offered in his broadcasts from WRR Dallas, but he bowed to the demands of the jukebox trade for hot Western Swing, and the basic lineup of the Cowboy Ramblers was augmented at his recording sessions with players from other bands, like fiddlers Jesse Ashlock and J. R. Chatwell, or pianist Smoky Wood.

Actually, "augmented" doesn't quite fit the case—often, Bill and brother Jim (1914–93) were simply the singers fronting another (uncredited) band entirely: the Modern Mountaineers in 1936, **the Light Crust Doughboys** at three long sessions in 1937–38, the Sons of the West in 1940. What the customers slipping nickels into the jukeboxes heard was not so much a Boyd band as a Boyd *brand*—a guarantee of hot 'n' happy swing music, varied with Western songs, waltzes, and lots of blues.

Bill managed his career skillfully, having a stint as an actor in Western B movies (though he isn't the Bill Boyd who played Hopalong Cassidy) and then becoming a DJ on WRR. Jim, a more instinctive swing musician, sang with Roy Newman's band and the Light Crust Doughboys.

You got good value in 1944: eighty-six songs, plus photo spreads and a life history, for seventy-five cents. The M. M. Cole company published innumerable hillbilly song folios in the '30s and '40s.

CLIFF BRUNER

Dates: Clifton Lafayette Bruner, b. April 25, 1915, Texas City, TX; d. August 25, 2000, Houston, TX
Instruments: fiddle, tenor guitar, vocals
Recording Debut: March 3, 1936 [with Milton Brown's Brownies]

KEY RECORDINGS

It Makes No Difference Now, **1938**
When You're Smiling, **1938**
Truck Driver's Blues, **1939**
Jessie, **1939**
Draft Board Blues, **1941**

When young Cliff Bruner joined **Milton Brown**'s Brownies in the summer of 1935, he added a sharp swing accent to the band's sound. We don't know how he learned to play like that. Fiddlers of his generation were often keen students of jazz players like Joe Venuti or Stuff Smith, whom they heard on radio and records, but Cliff, who came from a hardscrabble background, would have had little time or cash for either. His first playing, in his teens, was with traveling medicine shows.

When the Brownies broke up after Milton's death, Cliff stayed with the same label, Decca, leading first his Texas Wanderers and then, simply, "His Boys." In contrast to the big-band grandeur of **Bob Wills**'s Texas Playboys, Bruner's groups, like many others on the Texas swing-band scene of the '30s and '40s, mirrored what was happening in contemporary small-group jazz. Lead instruments—typically fiddle, electric steel guitar, electric mandolin, and piano—soloed by turns over a firm, drumless rhythm. Bruner's recordings from 1938–40, such as "When You're Smiling," with pianist/singer Moon Mullican and the imaginative steel guitarist **Bob Dunn**, vividly embody this concept of small-scale jazz with a Southwestern accent.

Bruner spent the '40s gigging around Texas, but in 1950, when his wife died and he had daughters to raise, he quit the road and became an insurance salesman. With a revival of interest in Western Swing in the '70s and '80s, he made a modest comeback, still a master fiddler. "There wasn't a night that went by," one of his latter-day bandsmen told me, "that he didn't play something that just amazed me." He recorded an album with the Nashville studio musician Johnny Gimble—who had started out as a Western Swing fiddler and was a longtime fan—and participated in Western Swing reunions.

Cliff Bruner on KPAC, Port Arthur, Texas: "Red Hot Rhythm, 12:15 to 12:45 p.m., daily." The business card dates from the late '70s.

BOB DUNN

Dates: Robert Lee Dunn, b. February 5, 1908, Fort Gibson, OK; d. May 27, 1971, Houston, TX
Instruments: steel guitar, trombone, vocals
Recording Debut: January 28, 1935 [with Milton Brown]

KEY RECORDINGS

Song of the Wanderer [with Milton Brown], **1936**
Star Dust [with Cliff Bruner], **1939**
Stompin' at the Honky Tonk, **1939**
What's Bob Done? [with Bill Mounce], **1941**
Taking Off [with the Modern Mountaineers], **1941**

Bob Dunn was the Charlie Parker of Western Swing. He rejected the conventional tonality of his instrument, converting the Hawaiian sweet talk of earlier steel guitar playing into a contemporary American argot, all slurs and slides and stabs, shouts and murmurs. Unsatisfied by the familiar melodic contours of popular song, he redrew them with the hand of a jazz and blues player, his attack unpredictable, his ideas tumbling over each other. The fiddlers of Western Swing may be its most feted musicians, but Dunn was arguably its creative genius.

He began conventionally enough, learning by correspondence course with the Hawaiian guitarist Walter Kolomoku, but (somewhat like **Merle Travis**) developed a technique of damping the strings with his picking hand. His first engagement with a serious Western Swing band was in Fort Worth, with **Milton Brown**, where for two or three years he gave other steel guitarists a vision of the future. When the Brownies broke up, he worked with Roy Newman, then **Cliff Bruner**, and for a while (at least on records) with his own band, the Vagabonds. In these years (1937–39), his range encompassed funky tunes like "Graveyard Blues" and "Stompin' at the Honky Tonk," the red-hot swing of Bruner's "When You're Smiling," and the gorgeous Hawaiian-my-way lines of "Star Dust." One of his signature pieces was the instrumental "Taking Off," which he recorded with Brown, Newman, and finally the Modern Mountaineers, each time with more daring.

After World War II, Dunn was based mostly in Houston, often working with the swing fiddler Dickie Jones. Had he lived a little longer, until the Western Swing revival of the '70s, he might have been recognized earlier as a style-setter whose ideas had permeated the music of contemporaries and successors like steel guitarists Leon McAuliffe, Noel Boggs, and Billy Briggs.

Bob Dunn and friends at the El Toro Club in Pearland, Texas. *From left*: Hezzie Bryant (bass), Leo Raley (electric mandolin), Mancel Tierney (piano), Dunn (electric steel guitar), Fritz Kehm (drums). The amplification system shown was state of the art for the time.

ADOLPH HOFNER

Dates: b. June 8, 1916, Moulton, TX;
d. June 2, 2000, San Antonio, TX
Instruments: guitar, vocals
Recording Debut: October 22, 1936 [with Jimmie Revard & His Oklahoma Playboys]

KEY RECORDINGS

It Makes No Difference Now [with Tom Dickey's Show Boys], **1938**
Maria Elina, **1940**
Spanish Two-Step, **1940**
Cotton-Eyed Joe, **1941**
Sage Brush Shuffle, **1942**

The melting-pot theory of American cultural history is brought to exhilarating life in South Texas, in the bubbling cauldron of musical styles created by communities speaking English, Spanish, German, Polish, or Czech. Here, the bandleader Adolph Hofner mined musical ore from both the Old World and the New to produce a unique alloy of country crooning, polkas, and Western Swing.

Hofner spoke Czech as his first language and had early memories of polka bands playing for community dances, but in his teens, records introduced him to Hawaiian music and mainstream popular song. In the mid-'30s, inspired by the stringband swing of **Milton Brown** ("I even tried to sing like him"), he and his brother Emil (or "Bash"), who played steel guitar, joined Jimmie Revard's Oklahoma Playboys, who made many records for the jukebox trade, often with Adolph taking the vocals. He worked with other bands too and had a jukebox hit with Floyd Tillman's song "It Makes No Difference Now" with Tom Dickey's Show Boys. The A&R man Eli Oberstein, who signed him to Bluebird Records in the spring of 1938, knew of Hofner's liking for Bing Crosby and hoped to turn him into the Bing of Western music. It didn't catch on, and anyway, once America was at war with Germany, no one was going to make a name in country music if they were called Adolph.

The postwar era saw a revival of polka music in the Polish American, Czech American, and German American communities of Texas, and for years Hofner made a steady living playing old songs and tunes—everything from polkas and schottisches to the "Milk Cow Blues"—in settings drawn from the varied musical experience of more than half a century. He became a San Antonio institution and was sponsored for thirty years by another, Pearl Beer.

Adolph Hofner and his band on KTSA, San Antonio, Texas, 1942. That year, over two days in Hollywood, they recorded tracks ranging from the Western Swing instrumental "Sage Brush Shuffle" to "The Prune Song"—in Czech.

CINDY WALKER

Dates: b. July 20, 1917, Mart, TX; d. March 23, 2006, Mexia, TX
Instruments: vocals, songwriter
Recording Debut: August 23, 1940 [with Texas Jim Lewis]

KEY RECORDINGS

Dusty Skies [by Bob Wills], **1941**
Bubbles in My Beer [by Bob Wills], **1947**
Warm Red Wine [by Ernest Tubb], **1949**
You Don't Know Me [by Eddy Arnold], **1956**
Distant Drums [by Jim Reeves], **1966**

Walker began writing songs as a girl; at twenty-three, she sold one to Bing Crosby. Soon afterward, she signed with Decca, recording both under her own name and with Texas Jim Lewis. Her 1941 "Soundie" of "Seven Beers with the Wrong Man" was effectively the first country music video by a woman, and, for a spell, she was something of a cowgirl pinup. But her singing career always came second to her songwriting. She composed around fifty songs for **Bob Wills**, among them "Cherokee Maiden," "Bubbles in My Beer," and the unforgettable "Dusty Skies," in which a cowboy bids farewell to a landscape eroded beyond recognition or use: "*Hate to leave the old ranch so bare / But I got to be movin' somewhere.*" It is as true a memorial of its time and place as the "Dust Bowl Ballads" of Woody Guthrie.

For years, Walker made an annual trip to Nashville to pitch her compositions to publishers, who placed them with **Gene Autry**, Hank Snow, **Webb Pierce**, Jim Reeves, and other country stars. "Warm Red Wine," a hit for **Ernest Tubb**, was inspired, she said, by a verse from Proverbs: "*Look not thou upon the wine when it is red.*" Her greatest success was with "You Don't Know Me," written for **Eddy Arnold**, revived by Ray Charles on his groundbreaking 1962 album *Modern Sounds in Country and Western Music*. No country purist, she also wrote for '40s pop singers Patti Page and Jo Stafford, and in 1962 Roy Orbison had a hit with her "Dream Baby." She led a quiet small-town life in Texas with her mother, Oree, who helped with the melodies of her songs. In 1997, her huge contribution to the Western song folio was recognized when she was inducted into the Country Music Hall of Fame.

When Cindy Walker was voted into the Country Music Hall of Fame, Harlan Howard (no slouch as a lyricist himself) called her "country music's greatest living songwriter."

TED DAFFAN

Dates: Theron Eugene Daffan, b. September 21, 1912, Beauregard Parish, LA; d. October 6, 1996, Houston, TX
Instruments: steel guitar, vocals
Recording Debut: November 4, 1937 [with Shelly Lee Alley]

KEY RECORDINGS

Truck Driver's Blues [by Cliff Bruner], **1939**
Worried Mind, **1940**
Blue Steel Blues, **1940**
Born to Lose, **1942**
No Letter Today, **1942**

Like many country musicians, Ted Daffan was turned on to steel guitar by Hawaiian music. By his midtwenties, he was playing electric steel in Houston bands like Leon Selph's Blue Ridge Playboys. Lacking the jazz chops of inventive steelmen like **Bob Dunn**, he played "straight lead," but he was good enough to be hired, with his friend **Cliff Bruner**, for recording sessions in 1937–38 with Shelly Lee Alley's Alley Cats. He did some singing, too, but realized that no record company would be interested in an unknown vocalist without original material.

Dining late, after gigs, at roadside eateries, Daffan noticed their popularity with truck drivers, "and it occurred to me that if someone wrote them a song, they would play it [on the jukebox], even if it wasn't very good. So I wrote 'Truck Driver's Blues,' and they loved it." Bruner's band had the hit, and Cliff commissioned Ted to write more numbers for him.

The success of the first trucking song caught the interest of Okeh Records' Art Satherley, who signed Daffan's band in 1940. It proved an excellent investment because, two years later, Daffan wrote a pair of songs that, when coupled on one record, became one of the bestsellers of the era. "No Letter Today" encapsulated the misery of wartime separation, but "Born to Lose" ("*and now I'm losing you*"), sung from the farther shore of desolation by fiddler Leon Seago, evoked larger uncertainties. Twenty years later, Ray Charles sang it on his album *Modern Sounds in Country and Western Music*, one of scores of versions of an imperishable country standard. Daffan never equaled it, but he prospered for a few more years in California before returning to Houston, where he carried on writing songs like "Tangled Mind," a Top Ten record for Hank Snow in 1957.

Ted Daffan was a top-line star of Columbia Records, which released more than fifty singles by him in the '40s.

SPADE COOLEY

Dates: Donnell Clyde Cooley, b. December 17, 1910, Grand, OK; d. November 23, 1969, Oakland, CA
Instruments: fiddle, vocals
Recording Debut: March 12, 1940 [with Gene Autry]

KEY RECORDINGS
Shame on You, **1945**
Detour, **1946**
Oklahoma Stomp, **1946**
Swingin' the Devil's Dream, **1946**

Although many Western Swing fans agree with Waylon Jennings that "**Bob Wills** is the King," that was not how it seemed in the '40s. The phrase "King of Western Swing" was first attached not to Wills but to Spade Cooley. The keyword here is "Western": by then, the epicenter of hillbilly swing was Southern California, where Wills was a relatively recent arrival but Cooley had been playing with country bands since the late '30s. And whereas Wills's music had a fiery spirit distilled and matured in the Southwest, Cooley's Kool-Aid swing had a distinctly West Coast flavor. A trade paper called it "Western tunes with sweet swing arrangements."

Cooley grew up in Oregon, of part-Cherokee heritage, then in the '30s moved to California, where his dark good looks earned him bit parts in Western movies. In 1940–41, he played fiddle on records by **Gene Autry**, Texas Jim Lewis, **Roy Rogers**, Jimmy Wakely, and others. He formed his own band in 1941, and during World War II, like Wills, he played regularly for promoter Foreman Phillips—who staged, in addition to evening events, early-morning swing shift dances for workers in war-related industries who didn't leave their factories until after midnight. Cooley's 1945 record "Shame on You" was no. 1 on the country chart for two months. He built a following for his brand of sumptuous wide-screen Western Swing at the Venice Pier Ballroom, Riverside Rancho, and Santa Monica Ballroom, from which he broadcast a live televised show.

Cooley suffered personal problems in the late '50s, a period that ended calamitously in 1961, when he was convicted of murdering his wife, Ella Mae, and given life imprisonment. Eight years later, on a three-day parole to play at a benefit concert at the Oakland Auditorium, he collapsed onstage and died shortly afterward.

In *The Kid from Gower Gulch* (1950), Cooley plays a Western movie star . . . who can't ride or sing. He appeared in several dozen Westerns, sometimes as a stand-in for Roy Rogers.

TEX WILLIAMS

Dates: Sollie Paul "Tex" Williams, b. August 2, 1917, Ramsey, IL; d. October 11, 1985, Newhall, CA
Instruments: string bass, vocals
Recording Debut: 1945 [with Spade Cooley]

KEY RECORDINGS

That's What I Like About the West, **1947**
Smoke! Smoke! Smoke! (That Cigarette), **1947**
Suspicion, **1948**
Life Gits Tee-Jus, Don't It?, **1948**
Artistry in Western Swing, **1948**

Tex Williams's voice was warm with the optimism of postwar America. In songs like "That's What I Like About the West," he offers a wide-screen vision of promise and plenty—"*We got liquid sunshine, legal moonshine, Reno, Frisco, Tahoe / Man, you name it, and if we ain't got it . . . we'll get it!*"—to a soundtrack of lush orchestral country music. It's virile, confident stuff, and funny too, when Williams deploys his laidback talking-blues manner on **Carson Robison**'s "Life Gits Tee-Jus, Don't It?" or lists the pleasures and perils of tobacco in "Smoke! Smoke! Smoke! (That Cigarette)" (cowritten with **Merle Travis**), which held the top spot on the *Billboard* country chart for tracts of 1947.

During the first half of the '40s, Williams had been the main vocalist for **Spade Cooley**, singing on his hit recordings "Shame on You" and "Detour." When Williams was approached to record in his own name, Cooley fired him, whereupon band members like guitarists Smokey Rogers and Johnny Weis joined the singer in his new berth at Capitol Records. At first, Williams followed a fad for polkas, charting in 1946 with "The California Polka," but gradually he developed a style of symphonic swing in Cooley's grand manner, even outdoing his former employer when he translated the jazz orchestra leader Stan Kenton's "Artistry in Swing" into Western Swing, replacing brass and reeds with accordion, steel guitar, and fiddles.

For much of the '50s, Williams worked in movies and on TV, but he began to show up in the country charts again in the late '60s and '70s, now an entertainer at Vegas or Reno but still unreeling tall tales against a Western Swing backdrop, as in that perennial favorite of they-don't-write-'em-like-that-anymore lists, "The Night Miss Nancy Ann's Hotel for Single Girls Burned Down" (1971).

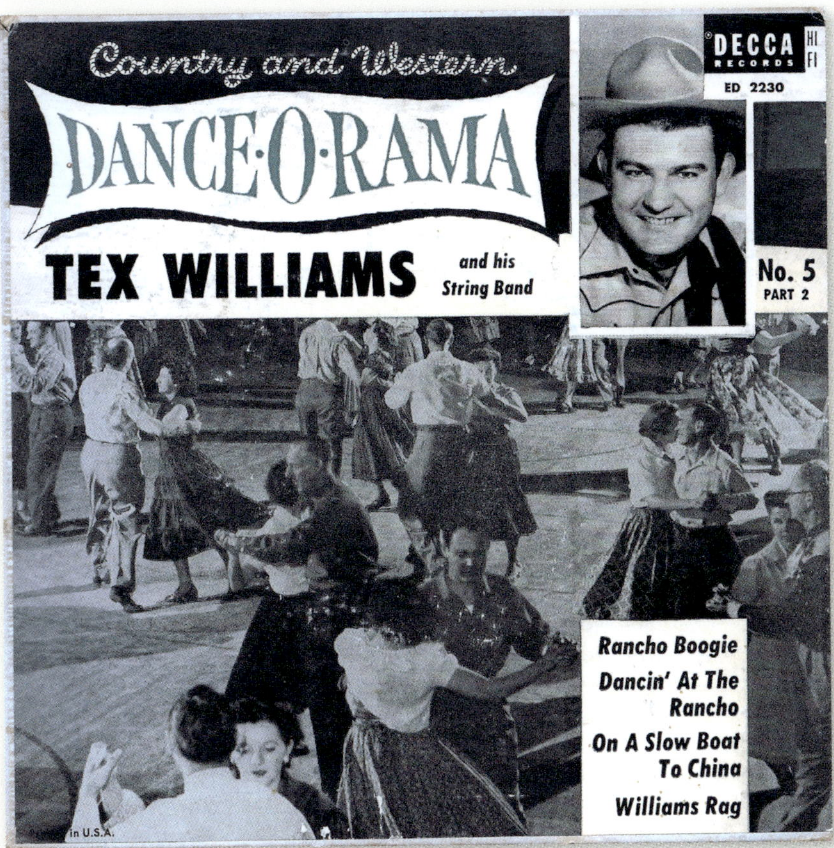

After his time with Capitol Records, Williams spent the early '50s with Decca, bringing them the snappy swing of "Roses and Revolvers" and the mystery story of "River of No Return." With its "Dance-O-Rama" series, Decca Records acknowledged its role as a primary producer of Western Swing since the '30s, issuing 10 inch LPs by Williams, Milton Brown, Bob Wills, Spade Cooley, Adolph Hofner, and other swing stars.

HANK PENNY

Dates: Herbert Clayton Penny, b. September 17, 1918, Birmingham, AL; d. April 17, 1992, Camarillo, CA
Instruments: guitar, banjo, vocals
Recording Debut: November 9, 1938

KEY RECORDINGS

She's Just That Kind, **1938**
Won't You Ride in My Little Red Wagon, **1939, 1950**
Bloodshot Eyes, **1949**
Hillbilly Be-Bop, **1949**
Jersey Bounce, **1950**
Tuxedo Junction, **1950**

Hank Penny was one of the most sophisticated musicians to work in the field of Western Swing. Unlike **Bob Wills, Milton Brown**, and most other first-generation bandleaders, he was not a Southwesterner, but he heard swing music as a teenager and straightaway fell under its spell. Inspired in particular by Brown, he formed his own version of the Musical Brownies, his Radio Cowboys, in 1938, and the following year they gained a spot on WSB Atlanta's *Crossroads Follies*. Tracks from that time like "Red Hot Papa" and "Won't You Ride in My Little Red Wagon" feature steel guitarist Noel Boggs and fiddler Boudleaux Bryant (later a successful Nashville songwriter with his wife, Felice).

In 1942, Penny moved to Cincinnati, Ohio, where he worked on WLW's *Boone County Jamboree* and *Midwestern Hayride*; then, in 1945, he was drawn to California by its thriving Western Swing scene. The powerhouse band he built there with players like **Merle Travis** and steel guitarists Speedy West and Herb Remington might have given **Spade Cooley** a run for his money. A long association with King Records produced "Bloodshot Eyes," written by Penny and later a hit for the Black singer Wynonie Harris, and the cool jazz of "Hillbilly Be-Bop" and "Tuxedo Junction," along with a revival of blues singer Tampa Red's "Let Me Play with Your Poodle." In 1949, he opened the Palomino Club, giving a Hollywood home to both country music and jazz. During the '50s, now recording for RCA Victor and Decca, he promoted the singing career of his wife Sue Thompson (who had pop hits in the '60s) and wrote humorous numbers like "Taxes, Taxes" that reflected his other career in stand-up comedy, which he pursued in Las Vegas and on the West Coast after he gave up full-time bandleading.

Hank Penny in his King days. He stoutly defended his vision of Western Swing as hillbilly jazz, and he faced up to King honcho Syd Nathan and West Coast promoter Foreman Phillips when they tried to sedate his music.

PEE WEE KING

Dates: Julius Frank Anthony Kuczynski, b. February 18, 1914, Abrams, WI; d. March 7, 2000, Louisville, KY
Instrument: accordion
Recording Debut: 1948?

KEY RECORDINGS
Tennessee Waltz, **1948**
Bonaparte's Retreat, **1950**
Slow Poke, **1952**
Bimbo, **1954**

The best-known fact about Pee Wee King is that he made the "Tennessee Waltz." The second best? That he was the first bandleader allowed to bring drums to the *Grand Ole Opry*. (It's said that when **Bob Wills** tried it and was forbidden, he walked out, never to return.)

But there is a small irony about "Tennessee Waltz": when it gave King the hit of his career, he had exchanged Nashville for Louisville. He was a Tennessean only by association. His roots were in Polish American Wisconsin, and what he first played, in high school and then on Midwestern radio, was polka music. In Louisville in the '30s, he absorbed the stringband swing of fellow WHAS act **Clayton McMichen**'s Georgia Wildcats and "got into the Western end of the business." In 1937, he and his Golden West Cowboys joined the *Opry*, his sound now less Polish than polished.

King's story of his big hit was that they were driving home from a gig when they heard **Bill Monroe** on the radio, singing his "Kentucky Waltz." No one, King's right-hand man, Redd Stewart, observed, had recorded a "Tennessee Waltz." By the time they reached Nashville, they had a song. The tune was one they already played, the "No Name Waltz." The lyric was a cautionary tale: Don't take your partner to a dance, or they may meet a wily waltzer. Stewart and King wrote it on a matchbook cover. Patti Page's pop cover was a chart-topping million-seller, and the song has since been recorded by everyone from Elvis to Ella Fitzgerald to Otis Redding. In 1965, it was officially declared the state song of Tennessee.

In the '60s, King went into the business end of the business, booking acts for county fairs. He was elected to the Country Music Hall of Fame in 1974.

Not just a star on records and the *Grand Ole Opry*, King appeared in movies with Gene Autry and had several national TV shows in the '50s and '60s.

HANK THOMPSON

Dates: Henry William Thompson, b. September 3, 1925, Waco, TX; d. November 6, 2007, Keller, TX
Instruments: guitar, harmonica, vocals
Recording Debut: 1946

KEY RECORDINGS
Whoa, Sailor, **1946, 1948**
Humpty Dumpty Heart, **1948**
Green Light, **1948**
The Wild Side of Life, **1952**

Inspired by the big-band Western Swing of **Bob Wills** and **Spade Cooley**, Hank Thompson skillfully applied its jazzy color to honky-tonk songs of heartbreak and hard drinking.

After serving in the US Navy during World War II, he took on the radio persona of "Hank, the Hired Hand" in his hometown of Waco, Texas, and recorded for independent labels such as Blue Bonnet and Globe. The regional success of "Whoa, Sailor" led him to Capitol Records, where he promptly had hits with "Humpty Dumpty Heart," a new "Whoa, Sailor," and "Green Light," revealing a talent for urbane, witty songs. The songwriter Harlan Howard praised him for "not being afraid to find unusual ways of saying things," but it was someone else's song that established him. Following the melodic contours of **the Carter Family**'s "I'm Thinking Tonight of My Blue Eyes" and **Roy Acuff**'s "Great Speckled Bird," "The Wild Side of Life," with its chorus beginning "*I didn't know God made honky-tonk angels*," dominated the country charts for more than three months in 1952.

Thompson became well known on TV and put country music on the menu at resort hotels in Nevada. *At the Golden Nugget*, made in Las Vegas in 1960, was one of the first country albums to be recorded live. He was admired for his compositions, his appealing voice, and the mellow swing of his Brazos Valley Boys, *Billboard* poll winners as the best country band for an unmatched fourteen successive years. With his models Wills and Cooley gone, he inherited the title "King of Western Swing"—a crown he wore with pride on his 1976 album *Back in the Swing of Things*. More than twenty years later, the album *Real Thing: Hank Thompson and Friends*—featuring duets with George Jones, Lyle Lovett, and others—proved he was still in the swing.

Hank Thompson was elected to the Country Music Hall of Fame in 1985 and the Nashville Songwriters Hall of Fame in 1997. The inscription on the photo is to fellow artist Cliff Bruner, also featured in this book.

WSM
NBC

HONKY-TONK & HEART SONGS

Most of the old-time singers of the 1920s and '30s preserved an Edenic vision, or illusion, of an untrammeled frontier life in mountain and hollow, held secure by the bonds of family loyalty and old-time religion. Their successors gazed upon a different world, a Depression-scarred but relentlessly industrialized landscape of strip mines and oil wells, roadhouses and dance halls, jukeboxes and casual pickups: rootless, secular, hyperreal. It called for a new music, and it found it in honky-tonk, which presented life seen through a long-haul trucker's rain-streaked window, or, at the end of the day, the bottom of his whiskey-streaked glass.

BUDDY JONES

Dates: Oscar Bergen Jones, b. December 25, 1902, Asheville, NC; d. October 20, 1956, Shreveport, LA
Instruments: guitar, harmonica, vocals
Recording Debut: May 26, 1931 [with Jimmie Davis]

KEY RECORDINGS

I'll Get Mine Bye and Bye, **1938**
She's Sellin' What She Used to Give Away, **1938**
Rockin' Rollin' Mama, **1939**
Settle Down Blues, **1939**
Mean Old Sixty Five Blues, **1940**

By the later '30s, Western Swing and what would later be called honky-tonk were the dominant sounds of Southwestern blue-collar entertainment, in clubs, in dance halls, and on jukeboxes. When recording crews rolled up in Dallas, Houston, or San Antonio, it was not just to cater for record buyers but for the operators of jukeboxes, wherever they were located, in taverns or bus stations, barbershops or amusement arcades. The nickelodeon could turn a record into a hit quicker than any number of broadcasts or personal appearances. Record companies pinpointed new releases judged to have jukebox potential and promoted them as "Operator's Specials."

One of the beneficiaries of the 'box was a genial Shreveport cop named Buddy Jones. His sun-warmed, cactus-dry delivery favored almost any material, from the downbeat "I Wish I'd Never Met You" to a cover of a **Jimmie Rodgers** song, but he specialized in blues and suggestive numbers like "She's Sellin' What She Used to Give Away." Accompanied by top Western Swing musicians like **Cliff Bruner**, **Moon Mullican**, and electric mandolinist Leo Raley, with his brother Buster Jones on steel guitar, his records either swung or dug into the lowdown groove of "Settle Down Blues." Whatever, it was great value for a nickel.

Jones had gotten into the record business through **Jimmie Davis**, playing the part of a musical hobo in his 1931 narration "The Davis Limited." Davis procured him a job as a Shreveport policeman and employed him in his broadcasting band—favors Jones may have returned by writing songs that Davis could copyright in his own name, like "I'll Get Mine Bye and Bye." He likely originated the scurrilous tall tale "Huntin' Blues" ("*We went huntin' the other night, me and my girl without a light*"), revived in the '50s as "Swamp Root" by the eccentric rockabilly Harmonica Frank.

Buddy Jones spent years as a sidekick to Jimmie Davis, but in the '30s his records had a wit and bluesiness all their own. This one, from 1939, features an early appearance of the term "rock 'n' roll."

MOON MULLICAN

Dates: Aubrey Mullican, b. March 29, 1909, Polk County, TX; d. January 1, 1967, Beaumont, TX
Instruments: piano, vocals
Recording Debut: November 20, 1936 [with the Blue Ridge Playboys]

KEY RECORDINGS

Pipe Liner's Blues, **1940, 1952**
New Jole Blon, **1946**
I'll Sail My Ship Alone, **1949**
Cherokee Boogie, **1951**
Moonshine Blues, **1951**

Country music has an abiding interest in the work that people do and the places where they do it. "Cotton Mill Colic" and "Weave Room Blues" describe the labor of weavers and doffers in textile mills, "Blackland Farmer" and "Down on Penny's Farm" the toils of agricultural workers. Other occupations have prompted "Mule Skinner Blues," "Wichita Lineman," and "Brakeman's Blues." **Ted Daffan**'s "Truck Driver's Blues," first recorded by **Cliff Bruner** in 1939, fronts a convoy of trucking songs that has run ever since. And in the oilfields of the Southwest, diggers and drillers found their theme song in "Pipe Liner's Blues." In the spring of 1940, its composer succeeded in selling it to three labels in quick succession, recording it with the Modern Mountaineers, the Texas Wanderers, and the Sunshine Boys.

He was the singer and pianist "Moon" Mullican, who had been playing since his teens, inspired by African American pianists he had heard in the barrelhouses of East and South Texas—men he may be remembering in his piano feature "Moonshine Blues." He took that music into the taverns of Houston, where, as he liked to say, "Music don't count if it don't make the bottles bounce on the table." He worked with many Texas swing bands but especially in the Houston–Beaumont area with Bruner, singing everything from "When You're Smiling" to "Kangaroo Blues." Later, he hooked up with King Records, where his ability to handle any kind of song enabled him to build a wildly diverse catalog, from the pseudo-Cajun "New Jole Blon" to the sugarcoated "Sweeter Than the Flowers," and from a remake of "Pipe Liner" to his career hit "I'll Sail My Ship Alone." His voice had heft and heart, and he stands, too little recognized, among the finer country singers of his time.

Moon Mullican on Nashville's WSM. His recording "New Jole Blon"—a pastiche of the old Cajun song "Jolie Blonde"—was pronounced the second-best hillbilly record of 1947 by the trade magazine *Cash Box*.

ERNEST TUBB

Dates: b. February 9, 1914, near Crisp, TX;
d. September 6, 1984, Nashville, TN
Instruments: guitar, vocals
Recording Debut: October 27, 1936

KEY RECORDINGS

Walking the Floor over You, **1941**
Soldier's Last Letter, **1944**
Tomorrow Never Comes, **1945**
Rainbow at Midnight, **1945**
Slippin' Around, **1949**

There was nothing fancy about Ernest Tubb. He sang as a plain man speaking plainly about things that concern us all: love and loss, happiness and sorrow, regret and recovery. He grew up in a small town in Texas, spending much of his youth under the storm cloud of the Depression. Idolizing **Jimmie Rodgers**, he replicated him on his San Antonio radio show, encouraged by Rodgers's widow, Carrie, and, at twenty-two, he recorded tributes to his model, accompanying himself on one of Jimmie's guitars. When a tonsillectomy robbed him of his yodel, he closed the Rodgers folio and began to sing songs written by himself and others. "Walking the Floor over You" was a regional jukebox hit, as were "Soldier's Last Letter" and "Tomorrow Never Comes." Typically, his vocals were unfussily accompanied by rhythm guitar and bass, with electric guitar providing decorative detail.

An invitation to join the *Grand Ole Opry* in 1944 had given him the chance to become a Nashville personality, and in 1947 he opened a record store there on Lower Broadway, mere yards from the *Opry* stage in the Ryman Auditorium. It was the location for his WSM show *Midnight Jamboree*, broadcast on Saturdays after the *Opry*, which introduced many up-and-coming country acts. The store and the program (now both gone) became fixtures of the Nashville experience, but its founder was often absent, since he kept up a relentless schedule of engagements. Not only did his stubbornly old-fashioned style appeal to folk who had grown up with it, but he found new admirers in the '70s and '80s among the "outlaw music" crowd.

Tubb's son Justin (1935–98) followed him into country music as a DJ, singer, and songwriter, delighting country music conservatives with his 1981 composition "What's Wrong with the Way We're Doing It Now."

Ernest Tubb in 1943 with guitarist Harold Bradley and bass-playing comedian Vernon “Toby” Reese.

BILL NETTLES

Dates: William Fletcher Nettles, b. March 13, 1902/1903, Natchitoches, LA; d. April 5, 1967, West Monroe, LA
Instruments: mandolin, vocals
Recording Debut: June 22, 1937

KEY RECORDINGS

Shake It and Take It, **1937**
Fannin' Street Blues, **1941**
I Feel the Draft Coming On, **1941**
Hadacol Boogie, **1949**
Hadacol Bounce, **1949**

At the start of his career, Bill Nettles seems to have enjoyed the patronage of **Jimmie Davis,** perhaps because he sold or shared his rights to songs Davis could use. (Some historians believe he wrote or cowrote Davis's huge hit "Nobody's Darling but Mine.") From the late '30s, based (like Davis) in Shreveport, Bill and his brothers Norman (1914–75), who sang and played guitar, and Luther (1909–98), on bass, together with fiddler "Doc" Massey, were heard over KWKH and on Vocalion discs like "Shake It and Take It" and "Oxford (Miss.) Blues," good-time numbers updating the spirit of **Jimmie Rodgers**. The addition of clarinet and accordion gave some of their later sides an air of Western Swing, but the group's style solidified with their 1941 recordings for Bluebird. Steel guitar and the deep-blue fiddling of the underrated Lonnie Hall seem to form a template for the ensemble sound of **Hank Williams**'s Drifting Cowboys, who would surely have heard the Nettles band on KWKH before they themselves joined its *Louisiana Hayride* in 1948.

In the late '40s, Bill tied his wagon to the *Hadacol Caravan*, a popular touring troupe featuring many hillbilly acts. To attend the show, a customer just had to produce a box top of Hadacol, a patent medicine promoted by Louisiana senator Dudley J. LeBlanc. "What was it good for?" LeBlanc was once asked. His reply was succinct: "Good for five million dollars last year." The appeal of the unpleasant-tasting brown brew was that it contained 12 percent alcohol: good news in dry counties. Hillbilly and blues musicians found it a ready subject for songs—and Bill's two for Mercury Records, "Hadacol Boogie" and "Hadacol Bounce," were hits—but, like many other down-home hillbilly acts in the '50s, he was sidelined by rock 'n' roll.

Bill Nettles (*standing, center, with mandolin*) and a lineup of the Dixie Blue Boys from the 1940s or '50s. With its mixture of hot music and hard sell, the *Hadacol Caravan* was perhaps the last of the great American medicine shows.

HANK WILLIAMS

Dates: Hiram King Williams, b. September 17, 1923, Mount Olive, AL; d. January 1, 1953, Oak Hill, WV
Instruments: guitar, vocals
Recording Debut: December 11, 1946

KEY RECORDINGS

Lovesick Blues, **1949**
I'm So Lonesome I Could Cry, **1949**
Cold, Cold Heart, **1951**
I Can't Help It (If I'm Still in Love with You), **1951**
Jambalaya, **1952**
Your Cheatin' Heart, **1952**

Whether as songwriter or singer, Hank Williams is the formative genius of modern country music. Like **Jimmie Rodgers**, he saw beyond the boundaries of "old-time music," but whereas Rodgers turned his sights uptown, Williams remained a man of his class, true to his raising. Thanks to a poetic gift rooted in religious belief and unweakened by troubles—lifelong back pain, binge drinking, impulsive romantic attachments—he crystallized his feelings, and his listeners', in sharply lit images, drawn from commonplace speech yet made unforgettable by the precision with which he constructed them and the humanity with which he uttered them.

As a boy in Montgomery, Alabama, tutored by an African American street singer, Rufus "Teetot" Payne, he acquired an instinctive understanding of the blues, and his first hit, the wry "Move It on Over" (1947), was followed by others cut from indigo cloth: "Lone Gone Lonesome Blues," "Moanin' the Blues," "Honky Tonk Blues." With his Drifting Cowboys, he was a star of the *Louisiana Hayride*. Joining the *Grand Ole Opry*, he worked beside his models, **Ernest Tubb** and **Roy Acuff**, but his Nashville years were marred by drinking and fights with his wife, Audrey. He returned to the *Hayride*, now erratic from his reliance on painkillers. Yet, his songwriting was unimpaired, and mainstream singers were taking notice. He stood on the threshold of fame, but, said a friend, "Hank seemed to be on a path that someone else was directing. . . . I can't figure how it would have ended any other way." That way was death, from a mixture of prescription drugs and alcohol, in the back of his Cadillac, on the way to a gig. He had flared like a rocket in country music's sky and was just as short lived, but, three generations later, his afterglow is undimmed.

Pathfinder
★ NEWS MAGAZINE June 4, 1952 15 CENTS

Hank Williams, fireball with a guitar

Otto Rothschild

Country Music Comes to Town

Hank Williams never made it onto the cover of *Time* magazine, but he did win that accolade from *Pathfinder*, a national magazine in the same news-digest business.

LEFTY FRIZZELL

Dates: William Orville Frizzell, b. March 31, 1928, Corsicana, TX; d. July 19, 1975, Nashville, TN
Instruments: guitar, vocals
Recording Debut: July 25, 1950

KEY RECORDINGS

If You've Got the Money I've Got the Time, **1950**
I Love You a Thousand Ways, **1950**
Always Late (with Your Kisses), **1951**
Mom and Dad's Waltz, **1951**
The Long Black Veil, **1959**

Though today his star is faint on the sky map of country music, Lefty Frizzell was one of the most influential stylists of his era. His laidback timing and extravagant melisma made an indelible impression on Merle Haggard and, beyond, on country stars of the '80s and '90s such as George Strait and Randy Travis. Maybe, too, his vocal slides and swerves were echoed in the singing of Buddy Holly.

He began singing in the late '40s on small stations in Texas and Arkansas, his style rooted in those of **Ernest Tubb** and Tubb's hero, **Jimmie Rodgers**, eight of whose songs he would brilliantly refashion on his debut album *Songs of Jimmie Rodgers* (1951). By then, he had had a no. 1 hit with his compositions "If You've Got the Money I've Got the Time" and "I Love You a Thousand Ways," success he replicated the following year with another of his own songs, "Always Late (with Your Kisses)." The focal point of these records is his extraordinary voice; the accompaniments are economical, the most prominent instrument sometimes not steel guitar or fiddle but piano.

Despite this runaway start, and frequent appearances on the *Grand Ole Opry* and *Louisiana Hayride*, his career stuttered for much of the '50s, sparking into life again only in 1959 with "The Long Black Veil." This is one of country music's great tragic dramas (man goes to the electric chair rather than admit to an affair with his best friend's wife), and Frizzell's version (the first) is enshrined in the National Recording Registry. He had a further hit with "Saginaw, Michigan" in 1964, but it was his last. For some time, his reliability had been compromised by alcoholism, and his election in 1972 to the Nashville Songwriters Hall of Fame acknowledged achievements he could no longer match.

In 1952, Frizzell had four records in the top ten of the country chart, but within a few years rock 'n' roll would turn artists like him into forgotten men.

RAY PRICE

Dates: Ray Noble Price, b. January 12, 1926, near Perryville, TX; d. December 16, 2013, Mt. Pleasant, TX
Instruments: guitar, vocals
Recording Debut: 1949

KEY RECORDINGS

Crazy Arms, **1956**
My Shoes Keep Walking Back to You, **1957**
City Lights, **1958**
Heartaches by the Number, **1959**
The Same Old Me, **1959**
For the Good Times, **1970**

Price was only a couple of years younger than his mentor, **Hank Williams,** but in 1951 Hank was the biggest name in country music, Ray just an up-and-comer with some radio experience from the *Big D Jamboree* in Dallas. Williams liked him and invited him to join his touring show, and in 1952, when Hank was sacked from the *Grand Ole Opry*, Price took over his backing band, the Drifting Cowboys. He was poised to step into Williams's shoes, but that wasn't his aim.

In 1954, Price hired a new band, the Cherokee Cowboys, who gave his music a Western Swing flavor and a 4/4 shuffle rhythm that became known as "the Ray Price beat." During the late '50s, he introduced deathless numbers like "Crazy Arms," "City Lights," "Invitation to the Blues," and "Heartaches by the Number," which mapped the honky-tonk terrain of pain and disillusion, their bleak contours etched by fiddles and pedal steel guitar. His star faded in the '60s but brightened again when he had a no. 1 hit with Kris Kristofferson's song "For the Good Times." By the end of the '70s, he had more or less retired to his ranch to raise horses, but in 1980 he partnered with Willie Nelson on the hugely successful album *San Antonio Rose*.

Historian Charles Wolfe credited Price with "some of the most crystal-pure singing from country music's greatest era." Price himself said, "A lot of people don't think of the voice as an instrument, but that's what it is. And I worked hard on my instrument over the years." When he emerged from semiretirement again in 2007 to tour with Nelson and Merle Haggard, promoting their shared album *Last of the Breed*, he gave them both what Haggard called "a goddamned singing lesson."

Ray Price went to college in Abilene, Texas, where he also found a spot in 1948 on radio station KRBC's *Hillbilly Circus*.

MOLLY O'DAY

Dates: Lois LaVerne Williamson, b. July 9, 1923, Pike County, KY; d. December 5, 1987, Huntington, WV
Instruments: guitar, banjo, vocals
Recording Debut: December 16, 1946

KEY RECORDINGS

The Tramp on the Street, **1946**
When God Comes and Gathers His Jewels, **1946**
The Drunken Driver, **1946**
Poor Ellen Smith, **1949**
Teardrops Falling in the Snow, **1949**

Amid the emotional maelstrom of honky-tonk, Molly O'Day presented calm faith and stoic acceptance. The world of her songs was full of loss: lost love, as in "I Don't Care If Tomorrow Never Comes," and lost loved ones, like the dying children of "The Drunken Driver" and "At the First Fall of Snow." She delivered these stripped-bare narratives of life's risks and sorrows in a clear, unadorned voice, sometimes dueting with her husband, Lynn Davis (1914–2000), underscored by a fiddle and a mournful steel guitar.

She started out in radio at sixteen, with her brother Skeets Williamson's band, on WCHS in Charleston, West Virginia. After marrying Davis in 1941, she borrowed from a silent-movie actress the stage name Molly O'Day and moved on up in 1945 to WNOX Knoxville's *Mid-Day Merry-Go-Round*. Her first record, "The Tramp on the Street," predicted all that followed, being a story true to life, told with compassion and moral conviction. She had the direct sincerity of **Roy Acuff** and, even more, of **Hank Williams**. They met early in their careers, and he supplied her with half a dozen songs, among them the harrowing mortality plays of "Six More Miles" ("*to the graveyard*") and "Singing Waterfall."

The religious feeling expressed in her songs was genuine, and, in the end, it compelled her to quit the music business. She came off the road in 1949 and ceased making records after experiencing TB in 1952. Thereafter, based in Huntington, West Virginia, she and Lynn engaged in radio ministry. In the '60s, however, small companies twice persuaded her to record again. Her themes were unchanged, for so was the world that inspired them: men and women still died in wars, and drunken drivers still terrorized the roads. Life's evening train stood always ready to depart.

Molly O'Day was also an accomplished old-time banjo player, as she showed on songs like the murder ballad "Poor Ellen Smith."

WEBB PIERCE

Dates: Michael Webb Pierce, b. August 8, 1921, West Monroe, LA; d. February 24, 1991, Nashville, TN
Instruments: guitar, vocals
Recording Debut: 1949

KEY RECORDINGS

Wondering, **1951**
Back Street Affair, **1952**
It's Been So Long, **1953**
There Stands the Glass, **1953**
Slowly, **1954**
In the Jailhouse Now, **1955**
Honky Tonk Song, **1956**

With his expressive, hard-edged voice and bluesy intonation, Webb Pierce was custom built for honky-tonk music, and he became a leading exponent of the genre. In his youth an admirer of **Jimmie Rodgers** and **Gene Autry**, he began performing in public in his twenties, singing with his wife, Betty Jane, on a small Shreveport station. Moving up to the *Louisiana Hayride*, he fronted a band including pianist Floyd Cramer and guitarist Faron Young. After two years with the West Coast indie label Four Star, he signed in 1951 with Decca, where he quickly scored a hit with "Wondering" (a success more than a decade earlier for the Cajun singer Joe Werner with **the Hackberry Ramblers**). In 1952, he was invited to join the *Grand Ole Opry*.

Over the next few years, Pierce grabbed a handful of no. 1s on the country charts, foremost among them honky-tonk classics like "Back Street Affair" and the alcoholic's excuse "There Stands the Glass." "Slowly" foregrounded the then newish sound of the pedal steel guitar (played by Budd Isaacs), and Pierce had his longest-running hit with an old number learned from a Jimmie Rodgers record, "In the Jailhouse Now." *Cashbox* magazine named him "Number 1 Country Male Vocalist" from 1953 to 1956 and did so again in 1961–63. By the '70s, however, his unreconstructed honky-tonk style and his taste for extravagant stage wear made by the Hollywood tailor Nudie seemed a little out of tune with Nashville fashion, and he drifted into semiretirement. But if his music no longer drew the fans, the status symbols of his glory years did, and countless tourists admired his Pontiac Bonneville, upholstered with silver dollars (another Nudie custom job), and the guitar-shaped swimming pool at his Nashville home. He was elected to the Country Music Hall of Fame in 2001.

Webb Pierce had a longtime buddy in the country singer (and truckers' favorite) Red Sovine. They joined the *Opry* at the same time and recorded duets such as "Why, Baby, Why."

THE MADDOX BROTHERS & ROSE

Instruments: fiddle, harmonica, mandolin, guitars, vocals
Recording Debut: 1946

KEY RECORDINGS
Milk Cow Blues, **1947**
Philadelphia Lawyer, **1949**
At the First Fall of Snow, **1949**
Last Night I Heard You Cryin' in Your Sleep, **1949**
Sally Let Your Bangs Hang Down, **1949**
George's Playhouse Boogie, **1949**
Water Baby Blues, **1950**

These five brothers and a sister created some of the most riotous music ever called "country." Whether the song was serious or comical, the singer (usually Rose) did their stuff against a backdrop of backchat, laughter, and general hoo-hah. It was a performance style developed on radio, in their broadcasts during the late '30s from KTRB in Modesto and KFBK in Sacramento, and again after World War II in Modesto. (The family had migrated to California from Alabama during the Depression.) Between 1946 and 1950, Cliff (1912–49), Calvin (1915–68), Fred (1919–92), Don (1922–2021), Henry (1928–74), and Rose (1925–98), billed as "The Most Colorful Hillbilly Band in America," transferred the musical mayhem to records on the indie label Four Star. They performed blues, boogies, heart songs, **Hank Williams** songs, and even sacred songs, incidentally scoring a hit with Woody Guthrie's "Philadelphia Lawyer." Their sound was a jangly polyphony of fiddle, mandolin, guitars, and harmonica, enhanced by talented West Coast session guitarists like Roy Nichols and Jimmy Winkle, with Rose's strident voice arching over the music like a steel rainbow.

After moving to a major label, Columbia, in 1951, the Maddoxes gradually toned down the background fun, and Rose emerged as the star. The group featured on the KWKH *Louisiana Hayride*, broadcast out of Shreveport, but broke up in 1956. Rose maintained her profile into the '60s with hit records on Capitol like "We're the Talk of the Town" and "Loose Talk" with Buck Owens. She also, to the surprise of many, cut the album *Rose Maddox Sings Bluegrass*, on which she did just that, aided by **Don Reno** and an uncredited **Bill Monroe**. A comeback in the '70s led to more fine albums and to overseas tours on the rockabilly circuit, where she was revered.

The Maddox Brothers & Rose brought to their radio programs and records the brio of the barn dance and the high spirits of the hootenanny.

COWBOY COPAS

Dates: Lloyd Estel Copas, b. July 15, 1913, Adams County, OH; d. March 5, 1963, Camden, TN
Instruments: guitar, vocals
Recording Debut: 1945

KEY RECORDINGS

Filipino Baby, **1945**
Signed Sealed and Delivered, **1947, 1961**
Tennessee Waltz, **1948**
'Tis Sweet to Be Remembered, **1951**
Alabam', **1960**

Copas sang and played guitar on small Ohio stations in his teens, but he first made a name by accompanying a character known as "Natchee the Indian" (a.k.a. Lester Vernon Storer), who was vigorously promoted in the Midwest during the '30s as a "champion fiddler" in "contests" with rivals like **Clayton McMichen**. In the spirit of these often-phony events, "Natchee" and Copas, both natives of Adams County, Ohio, devised bogus backstories, the fiddler alleging he was born on an Apache reservation in Arizona and Copas declaring himself a former miner and moonshiner from Letterbox, Kentucky.

By 1938, Copas was on WLW Cincinnati's *Boone County Jamboree*. Moving to Nashville, he joined the *Grand Ole Opry* and sang with **Pee Wee King**'s band, but when he began making discs, it was back in Cincinnati for King Records. He first scored with "Filipino Baby," written by Bill Cox, a West Virginia singer and record maker popular in the '30s, and later with "Tennessee Waltz," written by his former employer King. But the song most closely associated with him is his own eloquent waltz-time composition "Signed Sealed and Delivered," in which the singer mails his heart to his lover, because "*without you it's no good to me.*"

In 1948, Copas was voted the nation's top country artist by *Cashbox* magazine, but his star dimmed, and it would be another decade before his career was revived by a contract with Starday, success on record with the country-chart-topping "Alabam'" and a new "Signed Sealed and Delivered," and a return to the *Opry*. It was with *Opry* colleagues that he played his last gig, a benefit concert in Kansas City for country DJ "Cactus Jack" Call. He died, with fellow artists Hawkshaw Hawkins and **Patsy Cline**, when the plane bringing them back to Nashville crashed in bad weather.

With over sixty singles, Cowboy Copas was one of King Records' leading country artists.

MERLE TRAVIS

Dates: b. November 29, 1917, Muhlenberg County, KY; d. October 20, 1983, Tahlequah, OK
Instruments: guitar, vocals
Recording Debut: 1943

KEY RECORDINGS

No Vacancy, **1946**
Divorce Me C.O.D., **1946**
Dark as a Dungeon, **1946**
Sixteen Tons, **1946**
So Round, So Firm, So Fully Packed, **1947**
Sweet Temptation, **1947**

Innovative guitarist, witty songwriter, singer, inventor—Merle Travis had enough talent to fuel four careers. Guitar players love him for the thumb-and-finger picking technique he popularized, in which the heel of the picking hand damps the strings for a "choking" effect. His album *Walkin' the Strings* (issued in 1960 but recorded ten to fifteen years earlier) is a virtuoso exhibition of "Travis picking" on country tunes, pop songs, and, especially, blues. Among friends who played like him was Ike Everly, father of the Everly Brothers; among the many who learned to do so were Chet Atkins and Doc Watson.

Joining **Clayton McMichen**'s Georgia Wildcats in 1937, and subsequently the Drifting Pioneers, put Travis in progressive bands in a pivotal place, Cincinnati, where he worked on WLW's *Boone County Jamboree* and, in 1943, launched the King Records catalog. He also joined King artists Grandpa Jones and **the Delmore Brothers** in the gospel group the Brown's Ferry Four. He briefly worked in Californian Western Swing bands while still playing on King sessions with **Hank Penny** and others. Signing with Capitol in 1946, he stepped forward as a singer and songwriter, composing not only his own hits but also "Smoke! Smoke! Smoke! (That Cigarette)" for **Tex Williams**. He staked his claim in the newly fashionable idiom of folk music with the album *Folk Songs of the Hills* (1947), which held his most enduring composition, the coal miner's sour commentary "Sixteen Tons" ("*And what do you get? Another day older and deeper in debt*").

He also devised a blueprint for the first solid-body electric guitar, later developed by Fender; appeared in the movie *From Here to Eternity* (1954); took part in the Nitty Gritty Dirt Band's *Will the Circle Be Unbroken* (1972); and recorded collaborations with guitar pals Atkins and Joe Maphis.

Merle Travis entered the Nashville Songwriters Hall of Fame in 1970 and the Country Music Hall of Fame in 1977.

WILMA LEE & STONEY COOPER

Dates: Wilma Lee Leary, b. February 7, 1921, Randolph County, WV; d. September 13, 2011, Sweetwater, TN
Dale Troy Cooper, b. October 16, 1918, Randolph County, WV; d. March 22, 1977, Nashville, TN
Instruments: guitar, banjo, vocal (Wilma Lee); fiddle, vocal (Stoney)
Recording Debut: 1947

KEY RECORDINGS

Thirty Pieces of Silver, **1949**
Legend of the Dogwood Tree, **1950**
Sunny Side of the Mountain, **1951**
Walking My Lord Up Calvary Hill, **1951**
Big Midnight Special, **1959**

When Wilma Lee and Stoney Cooper from rural West Virginia embarked on a country music career in the early '40s, they were following a trail blazed by acts like **Lulu Belle & Scotty** and Bob Atcher & Bonnie Blue Eyes. Their music, however, was rather different: not Pollyannaish affability but diamond-hard Appalachian realism. The songs that made their name were hewn from nature and the Bible: "Thirty Pieces of Silver," "Walking My Lord Up Calvary Hill," "Sunny Side of the Mountain." Wilma Lee brought to these, wrote country music historians Mary A. Bufwack and Robert K. Oermann, "a spine-tingling new female country sound, a throbbing, sobbing, thrilling, chilling delivery that would influence stylists for years to come." Wilma Lee put it more simply. "My style is just the old mountain style. I'm a country singer with the mountain whang to it."

In her teens, she sang with the Leary Family, who in 1938 represented West Virginia at the National Folk Festival. Stoney joined the group, and they married in 1941. They gigged and broadcast in various Midwestern and Southern cities before returning in 1947 to West Virginia and WWVA's *Wheeling Jamboree*, where they stayed for a decade. Transcriptions of their shows, sponsored by Carter's Little Liver Pills, were circulated to radio stations across the country, and these, along with their recordings for Rich-R-Tone, Columbia, and Hickory, made them a leading act in pre–rock 'n' roll country music.

In 1957, Lee and Cooper progressed to the *Grand Ole Opry*, where their tenure was terminated only by Stoney's death. Wilma received Establishment recognition, recording for the Library of Congress and being described by the Smithsonian Institution as the "First Lady of Bluegrass." She made albums in both bluegrass and older styles and continued to appear on the *Opry* until 2001.

Wilma Lee and Stoney Cooper's decade on WWVA in Wheeling, West Virginia, culminated in three years headlining the Saturday-night *Jamboree*, a show almost as widely heard as the *Grand Ole Opry*.

KITTY WELLS

Dates: Ellen Muriel Deason, b. August 30, 1919, Nashville, TN; d. July 16, 2012, Madison, TN
Instruments: guitar, vocals
Recording Debut: 1949

KEY RECORDINGS

It Wasn't God Who Made Honky Tonk Angels, **1952**
Paying for That Back Street Affair, **1953**
Making Believe, **1955**
I Can't Stop Loving You, **1958**
Heartbreak U.S.A., **1961**

There had been women in country music before Kitty Wells—we have met more than a dozen already—but none achieved what she did: definitively placing women in the major league of country artists. Without her blazing the trail, female stars who found fame in the '60s and '70s, such as Dolly Parton, Tammy Wynette, and Loretta Lynn, would have had a longer and harder journey to success. The turning point was Wells's "It Wasn't God Who Made Honky Tonk Angels," a heartfelt female response to **Hank Thompson**'s "Wild Side of Life": "*From the start, most every heart that's ever broken / Was because there always was a man to blame.*" Thompson's song had been no. 1 on the country chart for twenty-seven weeks; Wells's riposte did the same. No woman had had a country hit on that scale before.

Wells had begun her career in country radio in the late '30s, singing with the popular duet Johnnie & Jack. Johnnie Wright, whom she had married not long before, chose her stage name from the old song recorded by **the Pickard Family**. Popular on the *Louisiana Hayride*, in 1952 the trio graduated to the *Grand Ole Opry*. Wells was already making records in her own name, and "Honky Tonk Angels" was followed by similarly pitched emotional dramas: "Paying for That Back Street Affair," duets with **Red Foley** such as "One by One" and "As Long as I Live," and a second no. 1 with "Heartbreak U.S.A." By the mid-'60s, the hits were fewer, but the imperturbably dignified Wells, "Queen of Country Music," remained at the center of the Nashville establishment for years afterward. In 1976, she was elected to the Country Music Hall of Fame; in 1991, she was the first female country singer to receive a Grammy achievement award.

The Kitty Wells—Johnny Wright Family Show was widely syndicated on TV in the USA and Canada in the '70s. Wells also toured throughout North America and Europe.

PATSY CLINE

Dates: Virginia Patterson Hensley, b. September 8, 1932, Winchester, VA; d. March 5, 1963, near Camden, TN
Instrument: vocals
Recording Debut: January 5, 1955

KEY RECORDINGS

Walkin' After Midnight, **1957**
I Fall to Pieces, **1961**
Crazy, **1961**
She's Got You, **1962**
Sweet Dreams (of You), **1963**

Had she come up in a different time and not been Southern and poor, Patsy Cline's career might not have been in country music at all. As a teenager working in small-town clubs, she sang like Helen Morgan, a torch singer of the 1920s and '30s whose dark, almost tragic looks she seemed to have inherited. Another model was Kay Starr, a big-voiced singer of the '40s and '50s who had some success in country music but was at heart a jazz vocalist.

In the early '50s, Cline left Virginia for Washington, DC, then a country music center, where the promoter Connie B. Gay put her on his *Town and Country* TV show. She signed with the West Coast indie label Four Star but had little success, and the hit that would establish her didn't arrive until 1957. "Walkin' After Midnight," supervised by the Nashville producer Owen Bradley, was a low-lit lament that shared the atmosphere (as well as the studio sound) of songs like "Heartbreak Hotel" or "Lonely Avenue." (Kay Starr had recorded the song first, but hers was never issued.) Cline's vocal is exquisitely paced by steel guitarist Don Helms, a veteran of **Hank Williams**'s Drifting Cowboys.

In 1960, Cline was finally embraced by the *Grand Ole Opry*, and in 1961–62, she had a remarkable triad of hits both in country and pop charts: "I Fall to Pieces," Willie Nelson's song "Crazy," and "She's Got You." All became country music standards, incessantly covered by other artists, and "Crazy" has been placed on the National Recording Registry. Cline lived to see none of this, having died in the plane crash that also took **Cowboy Copas**. Her life was dramatized in the movie *Sweet Dreams* (1985), and her work has continued to move and motivate women in and beyond country music.

In 1980, the character of Patsy Cline, played by Beverly D'Angelo, featured prominently in the Loretta Lynn biopic *Coal Miner's Daughter*.

THE LOUVIN BROTHERS

Dates: Ira Lonnie Loudermilk, b. April 21, 1924, Section, AL; d. June 20, 1965, Williamsburg, MO
Charles Elzer Loudermilk, b. July 7, 1927, Henagar, AL; d. January 26, 2011, Wartrace, TN
Instruments: mandolin, guitar, vocals
Recording Debut: 1955

KEY RECORDINGS

When I Stop Dreaming, **1955**
I Don't Believe You've Met My Baby, **1955**
You're Running Wild, **1956**
Cash on the Barrelhead, **1956**
My Baby's Gone, **1958**

One of country music's most influential double acts, the Louvin Brothers shaped the sound of the Everly Brothers. Later, their work caught the imagination of Gram Parsons and, through him, Emmylou Harris, who has revived several of their songs.

Ira and Charlie Loudermilk grew up in the Sand Mountain area of northeastern Alabama, absorbing music from their parents; their father played banjo, and their mother was involved in Sacred Harp singing. In their teens, they sang on small stations in eastern Tennessee, graduating in 1947, now known as the Louvin Brothers, to WROL in Knoxville. In 1955, they joined the *Grand Ole Opry*, and in 1956 they had three Top Ten hits and released what would become their most famous album, *Tragic Songs of Life*. Much of their music was rooted in the eternal verities of Southern religion, expressed in songs like "The Family That Prays" and "Satan's Jeweled Crown" and the 1959 album *Satan Is Real*, whose cover featured Mephy himself.

They were successful at a time when traditional country music was threatened by rock 'n' roll, but the new music would eventually undo them. In 1958, their producer, Ken Nelson, believing that the mandolin sounded old-fashioned in an era of electric guitars, asked Ira to stop playing it on their records. Ira took this badly, and because of his heavy drinking, the brothers' relationship worsened, until, in 1963, they disbanded. Ira died in a car wreck two years later. It had been his piercing harmonies and diamond-hard mandolin breaks that gave their music most of its character, and he had composed many of their songs. Charlie, though aware he had been the junior partner, persevered with a career in country music, consolidating his position as a respected cast member of the *Opry* and recording busily until shortly before his death.

SHOW & DANCE

SAT. 8:00 P.M. MAR. 18

ADMISSION ADULTS $1.00 - CHILDREN 50c

W S M GRAND OLE OPRY

PRESENTS - IN PERSON

THE LOUVIN BROTHERS

CAPITOL RECORDS

ALSO EXTRA ADDED ATTRACTIONS

JIM & JESSE

AND THE VIRGINIA BOYS

SPONSORED ON TELEVISION BY MARTHA WHITE MILLS

Jim and Jesse McReynolds, who shared the bill with the Louvins at this 1961 concert, were a leading bluegrass act for several decades.

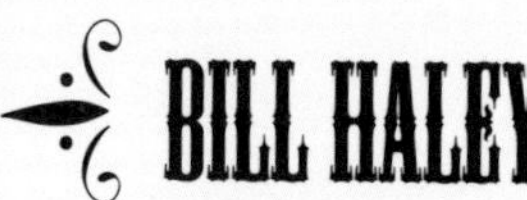

BILL HALEY

Dates: William John Clifton Haley, b. July 6, 1925, Highland Park, MI; d. February 9, 1981, Harlingen, TX
Instrument: guitar, vocals
Recording Debut: August 1948

KEY RECORDINGS

Rock the Joint, **1952, 1957**
Crazy Man, Crazy, **1953**
(We're Gonna) Rock Around the Clock, **1954**
Shake, Rattle and Roll, **1954**
See You Later, Alligator, **1956**

Rock 'n' roll changed almost everything, introducing new singers, new sounds, new songs, new energy, and a new audience. Established artists in country music were brusquely brushed aside. In barely five years, in the early to mid-'50s, the revolution was completed, the territory annexed, the business taken over. Pop music was in new hands.

That's the movie-script version. The real story is more nuanced. Even at the time, experienced listeners would have recognized rock 'n' roll as a composite of borrowings from earlier music: the takeoff guitar solos from Western Swing, the bellowing saxophone choruses from African American rhythm and blues, the energy of rockabilly, the rolling rhythms of country boogie-woogie, the nonchalant subject matter of happy-hour blues. There was much about rock 'n' roll that wasn't fresh-minted—and some of its proponents were no new kids on the block, either.

Take Bill Haley. This surprisingly key figure in rock 'n' roll, the man who gave the music an anthem in "Rock Around the Clock," was not some leather-clad teenage hip shaker but a genial thirty-something with a kiss curl who had made his name on the Pennsylvania country circuit, singing Western songs, billed as "the Silver Yodeler," and leading a band called the Four Aces of Western Swing. How he came to remake himself as a whiteface rhythm-and-blues singer remains somewhat mysterious, and it didn't work straightaway: On first release, "Rock Around the Clock" made little impression, but when featured in *Blackboard Jungle*, a 1955 movie about discontented high school students, it rocketed into the charts, in both the US and the UK, where both movie and song became touchpoints for rebellious teenagers. From 1954 to 1956, Haley's music was everywhere. But soon the hits stopped coming, and his last two decades were riddled with disappointment and drinking, occasionally relieved by rock 'n' roll veterans' shows.

Rock 'n' roll in the Pacific Northwest, 1957. But Haley's comet was soon to arc into a meteoric fall.

SACR
Don RENO
and Red S
WSM
WSM
On WRGP-TV Channel 3 - CHATTANOOGA, TENN.
MONDAYS 7:00 - 7:30 P. M.
STARS OF THE
GRAND OLE OPRY
FLATT
Earl

BLUEGRASS

Bluegrass was honky-tonk's straiter-laced cousin, similar in age but wholly different in outlook. Although the world around it was changing, bluegrass held out against modernity—both musically, by rooting itself in the sound of the old-time stringband, and lyrically, by reaffirming the values of family and landscape, the old cabin home, and the little white church in the valley. The aesthetic of its originators, **Bill Monroe** and **the Stanley Brothers**, set the rules: acoustic instruments, respectable stage wear, and fellowship with its audience. Eighty years on from its first appearance, some changes have proved irresistible, but bluegrass still embodies those founding principles.

BILL MONROE

Dates: William Smith Monroe, b. September 13, 1911, near Rosine, KY; d. September 9, 1996, Springfield, TN
Instruments: mandolin, vocals
Recording Debut: February 17, 1936

KEY RECORDINGS

What Would You Give in Exchange?, **1936**
(New) Mule Skinner Blues, **1940**, **1950**
Will You Be Loving Another Man?, **1946**
Blue Moon of Kentucky, **1946**, **1955**
Uncle Pen, **1950**

If it were possible to patent a musical genre, Bill Monroe would have owned bluegrass. No doubt its roots lay in Appalachian soil, in stringband music and harmonized vocal duets, but Monroe would have argued that bluegrass was his personal cultivar—a hybrid of old-time music, gospel quartet singing, and blues, with a strain of modern syncopation.

It took a decade to flower. As young men, Bill and his brother Charlie (1903–75) went north to work on WLS in Chicago and neighboring stations. In 1936, they joined the hillbilly roster on WBT in Charlotte, North Carolina, and made sixty intense mandolin/guitar duet recordings for Bluebird before they fell out in 1938—the first of several clashes that would redirect Bill's career. Now on the *Grand Ole Opry*, Bill created the first band he called the Blue Grass Boys, whose 1940–41 recordings like "Mule Skinner Blues" were a partial blueprint for the next stage. This came in 1946, when Monroe presented a dynamic new lineup, with singer-guitarist **Lester Flatt**, the game-changing banjoist **Earl Scruggs**, and fiddler Chubby Wise. Their high-energy renditions of "Blue Moon of Kentucky," "Molly and Tenbrooks," and other songs have passed into the bluegrass canon.

After Flatt and Scruggs left in 1948, a long succession of notable musicians became alumni of Monroe Academy: some were from similar backgrounds, like singer/guitarist **Jimmy Martin** and singer/banjoist Sonny Osborne; others were younger disciples, like banjoist Bill Keith, fiddler Richard Greene, and singer/guitarist Peter Rowan, from the college and folk-club milieu where Monroe found a new audience in the '60s. Though fiercely protective of what he saw as his creation, toward the end of his life he mended broken fences and played once again with peers like Ralph Stanley (of **the Stanley Brothers**) who did not dispute his title of "Father of Bluegrass."

Bill Monroe and the Blue Grass Boys on the *Opry* stage, 1951, with Jimmy Martin on guitar, Buddy Killen on bass, and Don Slayman on fiddle.

THE STANLEY BROTHERS

Dates: Carter Glen Stanley, b. August 27, 1925, Dickenson County, VA; d. December 1, 1966, Bristol, TN
Ralph Edmund Stanley, b. February 25, 1927, Dickenson County, VA; d. June 23, 2016, Coeburn, VA
Instruments: lead vocal, guitar (Carter); tenor vocal, banjo (Ralph)
Recording Debut: September 1947

KEY RECORDINGS

The White Dove, **1949, 1954, 1959**
I'm a Man of Constant Sorrow, **1951, 1959**
Angel Band, **1955**
How Mountain Girls Can Love, **1959**
Rank Stranger, **1960**

Ralph and Carter Stanley grew up in southwestern Virginia, near the Kentucky line—deep Appalachia, where music serves the serious purposes of remembrance, redemption, and release. Their mother, Lucy, played banjo, and their father, Lee, sang old-time songs. Broadcasts of the *Grand Ole Opry* sharpened the boys' ambition, and they began making music together, forming their first band in 1946. In 1947, they recorded for the eastern Tennessee independent label Rich-R-Tone, moving, in 1949, to a major, Columbia, where they presented tales of lost love and hard-won faith. Subsequently, they recorded for Mercury and King, their work keenly studied by the next generation of bluegrass musicians, among them Ricky Skaggs, who played mandolin with them as a teenager. In 1965, they appeared at one of the first bluegrass festivals, in Fincastle, Virginia; the following year, they toured Europe in a Festival of American Folk and Country Music.

Carter's death left the less outgoing Ralph uncertain how to carry on, but his Clinch Mountain Boys—with longtime members like fiddler Curly Ray Cline and guitarist George Shuffler, and a roster of distinguished lead singers such as Larry Sparks, Roy Lee Centers, and Charlie Sizemore—established themselves as a foundational bluegrass band. They played bluegrass festivals in the South and folk-music concerts in the North and recorded several albums a year for Rebel, from the influential gospel LP *Cry from the Cross* in 1971 to *Side by Side*, with Ralph's son Ralph II, forty-three years later.

In later life, Ralph found a new fan base, attracted by album projects uniting him with admirers like Bob Dylan, Emmylou Harris, and Alison Krauss, and by his role in the movie *O Brother, Where Art Thou?* (2000), singing the stark, a cappella lamentation "O Death."

Carter (*left*) and Ralph Stanley in their King days in the '50s. At the time, Columbia's budget label Harmony was still reissuing their classic recordings from the '40s like "The White Dove" and "The Lonesome River."

FLATT & SCRUGGS

Dates: Lester Flatt, b. June 19, 1914, Overton County, TN; d. May 11, 1979, Nashville, TN
Earl Scruggs, b. January 6, 1924, Flint Hill, NC; d. March 28, 2012, Nashville, TN
Instruments: banjo, guitar, vocals
Recording Debut: Fall 1948

KEY RECORDINGS

Foggy Mountain Breakdown, **1949**
Head over Heels in Love, **1950**
Flint Hill Special, **1952**
Randy Lynn Rag, **1955**
Crying My Heart Out over You, **1957**

Lester Flatt and Earl Scruggs were the first members of **Bill Monroe**'s Blue Grass Boys to make an independent, albeit joint, career—one in which they were, for a time, more prominent than their former employer. But their individual contributions to the genre began while they were with him. Flatt was a subtle singer and solid guitarist, inventor of trademark runs, while Scruggs carried in his fingers and banjo case the tools of a musical revolution, the creation of the intricate, accented, exuberant language of bluegrass banjo picking. (He was also a fine guitarist.) After four years with Monroe and Columbia Records (1944–48), they left to sign with Mercury and had a hit with "Foggy Mountain Breakdown," later heard in the movie *Bonnie and Clyde*. In 1951, in a double shuffle, they returned to Columbia while Monroe left for Decca, and for the rest of the '50s and into the '60s, they produced many instrumentals and vocal numbers, the latter often written by Flatt, that would become bluegrass standards.

The novelty song "The Ballad of Jed Clampett," written for the enormously popular TV series *The Beverly Hillbillies*, did most to spread their name, giving them the clout to take on ventures such as a concert at Carnegie Hall and—less to the traditionalist Flatt's taste—an album devoted to the songs of Bob Dylan. With their different notions of musical direction, a breakup was inevitable, and it came in 1969. Flatt continued to be a mainstay of the *Grand Ole Opry* (where the duo had first played, with Monroe, twenty-five years earlier), leading the Nashville Grass, while Scruggs, plus several sons, formed the Earl Scruggs Revue and devoted himself to the campus folk-club circuit, moving away from mainstream bluegrass and to some extent disowning his role in creating it.

Martha White was a longtime sponsor of the *Grand Ole Opry*. Flatt & Scruggs sang a jingle about the product during their slot on the show.

JIMMY MARTIN

Dates: b. August 10, 1927, Sneedville, TN; d. May 14, 2005, Nashville, TN
Instruments: guitar, vocals
Recording Debut: 1949 [with Bill Monroe]

KEY RECORDINGS

20/20 Vision, **1954, 1964**
You Don't Know My Mind, **1960**
Don't Give Your Heart to a Rambler, **1961**
Widow Maker, **1963**
Sunny Side of the Mountain, **1964**

Jimmy Martin had a gift: He brought to the soaring harmonies and dancing rhythms of bluegrass some of the earthbound solidity of honky-tonk. In 1949, he was engaged by **Bill Monroe** and in two spells with the Blue Grass Boys proved himself an adventurous guitarist and their finest lead singer since **Lester Flatt**. Between the Monroe gigs, he and banjoist Bobby Osborne recorded superb duets such as "Blue Eyed Darlin'," and in 1954–55 he and the Osborne Brothers formed the Sunny Mountain Boys, playing for transplanted Southerners in the Midwest and making exceptional recordings like "20/20 Vision" and "Save It! Save It!"

Thereafter, Martin concentrated on establishing his own reputation rather than augmenting other people's. (He had, in any case, a volatile personality that made him a rogue element in the chemistry of a strictly controlled band like Monroe's.) In 1956, he signed with Decca, made some noise with "Hit Parade of Love," and gathered around him long-stay colleagues like banjoist J. D. Crowe (who later led the influential band the New South, featuring the mold-breaking singer/guitarist Tony Rice) and mandolinist Paul Williams. It was one of the most precise but also soulful of bluegrass bands, and many of its recordings have become genre standards, such as "Rock Hearts," "Ocean of Diamonds," and, notably, "You Don't Know My Mind," "Don't Give Your Heart to a Rambler," and "Freeborn Man"—three skillfully wrought compositions by the now-little-remembered honky-tonk singer Jimmie Skinner.

Though working in bluegrass, Martin called his music "good 'n' country." It was a phrase he liked well enough to use as the title of an early album, but in the changing conditions of country music in the '60s, it was no guarantee of a lifelong audience, and after the '70s he was relatively inactive.

Jimmy Martin with his longtime companion and mother of his children, Barbara Stephens, backstage at the *Opry*, ca. 1951.

RENO & SMILEY

Dates: Donald Wesley Reno, b. February 21, 1926, Spartanburg, SC; d. October 16, 1984, Charlottesville, VA
Arthur Lee "Red" Smiley, b. May 17, 1925, Asheville, NC; d. January 2, 1972, Philadelphia, PA
Instruments: banjo, guitar, vocals
Recording Debut: January 1952

KEY RECORDINGS

I'm Using My Bible for a Roadmap, **1952**
Country Boy Rock 'n' Roll, **1956**
I Know You're Married, **1957**
I Wouldn't Change You If I Could, **1959**
Don't Let Your Sweet Love Die, **1961**

Reno was an adept lead guitarist, but he is better known for his technically sophisticated banjo playing, developed partly from older musicians he heard when growing up in North Carolina, like Snuffy Jenkins (who had played with **Mainer's Mountaineers**), and partly to avoid comparison with his contemporary **Earl Scruggs**, whom he replaced in **Bill Monroe**'s Blue Grass Boys in 1948–49. In 1950, Reno partnered with singer/guitarist Red Smiley, heading the Tennessee Cut-Ups, and in 1952 they began recording for King, their first hit being "I'm Using My Bible for a Roadmap." For a while, they were a records-only act, but in 1955 they went back on the road and became one of the most prominent bluegrass groups in the Southeast. The three albums *Sacred Songs*, *Instrumentals*, and *Instrumentals and Ballads*, all issued in 1958, show the extraordinary range of their material, from "Get Behind Me Satan" to "Hen Scratchin' Stomp" to "I'm the Talk of the Town." Among their most successful singles were "I Know You're Married" ("*but I love you still*") and "Don't Let Your Sweet Love Die," revived twenty years later by Ricky Skaggs.

In 1955, Reno was briefly reunited on record with a former employer. Arthur Smith had created the 1945 million-seller "Guitar Boogie" and was thereafter known as Arthur "Guitar Boogie" Smith to distinguish him from the *Grand Ole Opry* fiddler Arthur Smith. "Feudin' Banjos," devised by Smith, was a conversation between his four-string banjo and Reno's five-string. Seventeen years later, this catchy novelty, rerecorded by Eric Weissberg and Steve Mandell as "Dueling Banjos," was used for a memorably strange sequence in the movie *Deliverance*.

Red Smiley retired in 1965 for health reasons; for the next decade, Reno worked with singer/guitarist Bill Harrell (1934–2009), Smiley rejoining them for his last couple of years.

Don and Red don the blue and gray for one of their many themed EPs for King Records.

AFTERWORD

"Vintage country" didn't cease to exist when its original makers retired or died. In the '50s and '60s, young musicians, reacting to changes in country music and larger shifts in society, began to look back at earlier times and discover songs and tunes that had resonated with their forebears.

Many were shown the way there by the *Anthology of American Folk Music*, produced in 1952 by filmmaker and ethnologist Harry Smith: a set of six LPs reissuing eighty-four 78 rpm recordings by both Black and white artists from the 1920s and '30s. Among the musicians it inspired were the New Lost City Ramblers—Mike Seeger, John Cohen, and Tom Paley (later replaced by Tracy Schwarz)—who began to perform a larger legacy of recorded old-time and bluegrass music.

Not content with reinstating old repertoire, Seeger and Cohen began to rediscover the now-older men and women who had played it: some who had made records, like Dock Boggs, and others who hadn't, such as the singer, guitarist, and banjoist Roscoe Holcomb. Folkways Records issued LPs of these figures, while labels like County and Rounder reissued recordings from the old-time catalogs and made new ones of living folk heroes like Tommy Jarrell and E. C. Ball.

In parallel with this record-based activity, musicians from the North began to compete at long-established Southern events like the fiddlers' conventions in Galax, Virginia, and Union Grove, North Carolina, sometimes alongside men and women who had inspired them (or their descendants). Cliques of old-time musicians developed in Chapel Hill and Durham, North Carolina, the starting point for the Hollow Rock String Band, Fuzzy Mountain String Band, and Red Clay Ramblers, and in Ithaca, New York, home of the Highwoods String Band. In the '70s and '80s, groups like these influenced the sound and repertoire of stringbands everywhere.

This intense investigative interest in neglected music was not focused only on Southern old-time idioms. Bands played country-dance music

The three two-LP boxes of the *Anthology of American Folk Music* were redesigned in the '60s to feature a Depression image by the photographer Ben Shahn. A boxed six-CD set appeared in 1997 and won two Grammy awards the following year. Harry Smith, who died in 1991, once said, "I saw America changed through music." His *Anthology* played a major role in that change.

Roscoe Holcomb (1912–81) of Daisy, Kentucky, was the central subject of John Cohen's 1963 film *The High Lonesome Sound*. He made several remarkable albums for Folkways.

The Coen brothers' 2000 movie *O Brother, Where Art Thou?* and its Grammy-winning soundtrack album dramatically raised public awareness of old-time music and bluegrass.

Tracy Schwarz, Mike Seeger, and John Cohen—the New Lost City Ramblers—onstage at the Newport Folk Festival, 1966.

from New England, or fiddle tunes and styles peculiar to Ohio, Indiana, or Illinois. The spotlight swung to the Southwest and lit up a revival of Western Swing, many of whose original practitioners were still in their prime and relished the opportunity to play hillbilly jazz and honky-tonk music for a new audience.

On the West Coast, swing, honky-tonk, and bluegrass had already become a collective inspiration for the country rock of the Byrds and Gram Parsons. A later generation of musicians drawing on similar sources were the "new traditionalists" of the '80s and '90s, such as Ricky Skaggs, who came from bluegrass; Randy Travis, a honky-tonk legatee of Hank Williams and Lefty Frizzell; and the loose confederacy of alt.country.

Two generations further on, vintage country continues to excite new devotees, performers and listeners alike. Figures like Chris Stapleton or Sturgill Simpson keep alive in the Nashville milieu the spirit of honky-tonk or "hard country," while old-time and bluegrass musicians maintain vigorous tribal existences on their own circuits—boosted, from time to time, when vintage country breaks into the larger world of popular culture, to leave its unignorable stamp on movies like *Cold Mountain* or *O Brother, Where Art Thou?* Perhaps more than any other genre of Western popular music, country music listens—affectionately, attentively, and always creatively—to its own past.

INDEX

Page references in bold indicate artist entries.

SELECT BIBLIOGRAPHY

Some of these books can be found in later (often paperback) editions on Amazon and other online sites.

Beckworth, Josh. *Always Been a Rambler: G. B. Grayson and Henry Whitter, Country Music Pioneers of Southern Appalachia*. Jefferson, NC: McFarland, 2018.

Berry, Chad (ed.). *The Hayloft Gang: The Story of the National Barn Dance*. Urbana: University of Illinois Press, 2008.

Bufwack, Mary A., and Robert K. Oermann. *Finding Her Voice: Women in Country Music, 1800–2000*. Nashville: Vanderbilt University Press, 2003.

Cantwell, Robert. *Bluegrass Breakdown: The Making of the Old Southern Sound*. Urbana: University of Illinois Press, 1984.

Daniel, Wayne W. *Pickin' on Peachtree: A History of Country Music in Atlanta, Georgia*. Urbana: University of Illinois Press, 1990.

Doubler, Michael D. *Dixie Dewdrop: The Uncle Dave Macon Story*. Urbana: University of Illinois Press, 2018.

Dylan, Bob. *Chronicles Volume One*. New York: Simon & Schuster, 2004.

Escott, Colin, with George Merritt and William MacEwen. *Hank Williams: The Biography*. Boston: Little, Brown, 1994.

George-Warren, Holly. *Public Cowboy No. 1: The Life and Times of Gene Autry*. New York: Oxford University Press, 2007.

Ginell, Cary. *Milton Brown and the Founding of Western Swing*. Urbana: University of Illinois Press, 1994.

Green, Douglas B. *Singing in the Saddle: The History of the Singing Cowboy*. Nashville: Vanderbilt University Press, 2002.

Horstman, Dorothy. *Sing Your Heart Out, Country Boy*. 2nd edition, Nashville: Country Music Foundation Press, 1986.

Huber, Patrick. *Linthead Stomp: The Creation of Country Music in the Piedmont South*. Chapel Hill: University of North Carolina Press, 2008.

Jones, Loyal. *Radio's "Kentucky Mountain Boy" Bradley Kincaid*. Berea, KY: Appalachian Center, 1980.

Jones, Loyal. *Minstrel of the Appalachians: The Story of Bascom Lamar Lunsford*. Boone, NC: Appalachian Consortium Press, 1984.

Kingsbury, Paul, Michael McCall, and John W. Rumble (eds.). *The Encyclopedia of Country Music*. 2nd edition. New York: Oxford University Press, 2012.

Malone, Bill C., and Tracey E. W. Laird. *Country Music USA*. Fiftieth Anniversary Edition. Austin: University of Texas Press, 2018.

Mazor, Barry. *Meeting Jimmie Rodgers*. New York: Oxford University Press, 2009.

Mazor, Barry. *Ralph Peer and the Making of Popular Roots Music*. Chicago: Chicago Review Press, 2015.

Porterfield, Nolan. *Jimmie Rodgers: The Life and Times of America's Blue Yodeler*. Urbana: University of Illinois Press, 1979.

Reid, Gary B. *The Music of the Stanley Brothers*. Urbana: University of Illinois Press, 2014.

Rorrer, Kinney. *Rambling Blues: The Life and Songs of Charlie Poole (Old Time Music Booklet 3)*. London: Old Time Music, 1982.

Rosenberg, Neil V. *Bluegrass: A History*. Urbana: University of Illinois Press, 1985.

Russell, Tony. *Blacks, Whites and Blues*. New York: Stein & Day, 1970. Reprinted in Oliver, Paul, and others. *Yonder Come the Blues*. Cambridge: Cambridge University Press, 2001.

Russell, Tony. *Country Music Records: A Discography, 1921–1942*. New York: Oxford University Press, 2004.

Russell, Tony. *Country Music Originals: The Legends and the Lost*. New York: Oxford University Press, 2007.

Russell, Tony. *Rural Rhythm: The Story of Old-Time Country Music in 78 Records*. New York: Oxford University Press, 2021.

Stambler, Irwin, and Grelun Landon. *The Encyclopedia of Folk, Country and Western Music*. 2nd ed. New York: St Martin's Press, 1983.

Stanley, Dr. Ralph, and Eddie Dean. *Man of Constant Sorrow: My Life and Times*. New York: Penguin Books/Gotham Books, 2009.

Townsend, Charles R. *San Antonio Rose: The Life and Music of Bob Wills*. Urbana: University of Illinois Press, 1976.

Tribe, Ivan M. *The Stonemans: An Appalachian Family and the Music That Shaped Their Lives*. Urbana: University of Illinois Press, 1993.

Ward, Brian, and Patrick Huber. *A&R Pioneers: Architects of American Roots Music on Record*. Nashville: Country Music Foundation Press/Vanderbilt University Press, 2018.

White, John I. *Git Along, Little Dogies: Songs and Songmakers of the American West*. Urbana: University of Illinois Press, 1975.

Wiggins, Gene. *Fiddlin' Georgia Crazy: Fiddlin' John Carson, His Real World, and the World of His Songs*. Urbana: University of Illinois Press, 1987.

Wolfe, Charles K. *A Good-Natured Riot: The Birth of the Grand Ole Opry*. Nashville: Country Music Foundation Press and Vanderbilt University Press, 1999.

Zwonitzer, Mark, with Charles Hirshberg. *Will You Miss Me When I'm Gone: The Carter Family & Their Legacy in American Music*. New York: Simon & Schuster, 2004.

Online resources are too numerous to list. I recommend the website **Hillbilly-music.com**, which is devoted to assembling the myriad jigsaw pieces of country music history.

CREDITS

Unless otherwise stated, all images in this book are from the author's collection.

Archive Photos/Getty Images: 213
Bettman/Getty Images: 230
Donaldson Collection/Getty Images: 119
EBC/courtesy of British Country Music Association: 115, 125, 171B
GAB Archive/Getty Images: 67, 215T
Guthrie T. Meade Collection #20246, Southern Folklife Collection, Wilson Special Collections Library, University of North Carolina at Chapel Hill: 55B
Heritage Auctions: 151, 157, 163, 227, 229, 230BL, 237
Heritage Images/Getty Images: 35
John Byrne Cooke Estate/Getty Images: 244T
John Kisch Archive/Getty Images: 185
Ken McFarland: 43
Kev Coffey: 203T
Kinney Rorrer: 45
Leila Grossman/Getty Images: 223T, 230BR, 233T, 239
Lou Harshaw/Archive Photos/Getty Images: 91
Michael Ochs Archives/Getty Images: cover L, 2C, 141, 142BL, 159, 194BL, 194BR, 199, 207, 209, 217T, 219, 221, 225, 245
Norm Cohen: 39
Pictorial Press/Alamy Stock Photo: cover R, 2BR, 27, 181
Private collection: 57R, 233B, 235B, 244B
Public domain: 99
Rich Nevins: 85
Richard Weize: 201
Smithsonian Institution/National Museum of American History: 83
Smithsonian Institution/Folkways Recordings: 101T, 243
Underwood Archives/Getty Images: 149

ACKNOWLEDGMENTS

I'm grateful for the input—both indirectly, through their writings, and directly, in discussion and correspondence—of my friends and colleagues Kevin Coffey, Norm Cohen, Carl Fleischhauer, Cary Ginell, Doug Green, Patrick Huber, Lance Ledbetter, Bill Malone, Frank Mare, Wayne Martin, Rich Nevins, Robert K. Oermann, Ted Olson, Barry Poss, Ronnie Pugh, Kinney Rorrer, Ben Sandmel, Dave Sichak, Dick Spottswood, Malcolm Vidrine, Stephen Wade, and Marshall Wyatt.

I also remember the lessons I learned from now absent friends, among them Joe Bussard, John Cohen, Chris Comber, Wayne Daniel, Eugene Earle, David Freeman, Archie Green, Guthrie T. Meade, Bob Pinson, Nolan Porterfield, Art Rosenbaum, Mike Seeger, Chris Strachwitz, Ivan Tribe, Gene Wiggins, Joe Wilson, and Charles K. Wolfe.

My thanks too to family members and friends: Sharon Banoff, Ricky Russell, Sally Feldman, and Tony Engle.

I am grateful to Will Steeds and Laura Ward of the Elephant Book Company, who commissioned the book; to my always affable editor Tom Seabrook, who guided it expertly to publication; and to Scott B. Bomar for his foreword.

Tony Russell

AUTHOR BIOS

Tony Russell is an internationally recognized historian of early country music, the author of the award-winning *Country Music Records: A Discography, 1921–1942*, *Country Music Originals: The Legends and the Lost*, and other books on American vernacular music. Founder and editor of the magazine *Old Time Music*, he has also written for many other periodicals and has compiled and annotated several hundred albums of country music, blues, and jazz.

Scott B. Bomar is an award-winning writer, researcher, and music historian based in Los Angeles. He has authored or coauthored six books, including *The Byrds: 1964–1967* (with Roger McGuinn, Chris Hillman, and David Crosby), *Every Night Is Saturday Night* (with Wanda Jackson), *Johnny Cash at Folsom & San Quentin*, and the forthcoming *Bakersfield Sounds: The Rise and Fall of Country Music's "Nashville West."* Scott has earned three Grammy nominations in the category of Best Album Notes, including for his ten-CD box set *The Bakersfield Sound*. In 2024, he received the Chet Flippo Award for Excellence in Country Music Journalism.